# GAME CHANGERS

## The Greatest Plays in
# NEW ENGLAND
# PATRIOTS HISTORY

Sean Glennon

## TRIUMPH
### BOOKS

*To my home team: Mo and Seamus.*

Library of Congress Cataloging-in-Publication Data

Glennon, Sean, 1966–
  Game changers : the greatest plays in New England Patriots history / Sean Glennon.
    p. cm.
  Includes bibliographical references.
  ISBN-13: 978-1-60078-400-2
  ISBN-10: 1-60078-400-3
  1.  New England Patriots (Football team)—History.  I. Title.
  GV956.N36G53 2010
  796.332'640974461—dc22

                                      2010018851

This book is available in quantity at special discounts for your group or organization. For further information, contact:
  **Triumph Books**
  542 South Dearborn Street
  Suite 750
  Chicago, Illinois 60605
  (312) 939-3330
  Fax (312) 663-3557
  www.triumphbooks.com

Printed in China
ISBN: 978-1-60078-400-2
Design by Sue Knopf/Patricia Frey
Page production by Patricia Frey

# Contents

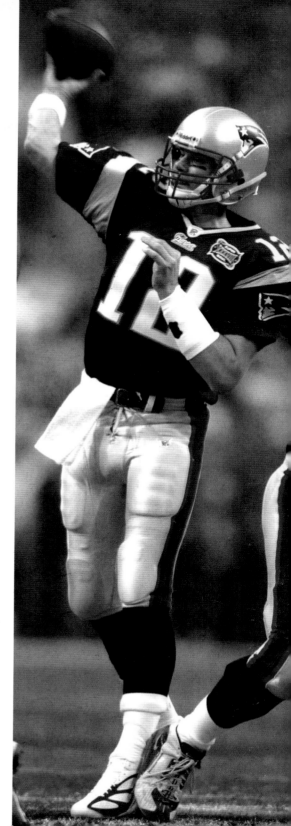

# Foreword

I was somewhat surprised when I was asked to write this foreword. With the great success of the Patriots recently and the great players on those teams, it was humbling to be asked to be part of a book that chronicles some of the most important plays in the franchise's 50-year history.

I was blessed to play 25 years of organized football. I started in the seventh grade and played through high school. I was red-shirted in college, which gave me an extra year of playing. Then I was drafted and played professional football for the Patriots for 14 years.

My favorite play from the time I was a 12-year-old seventh-grade linebacker until I was a 36-year-old pro linebacker was always when my quarterback would take a knee in the victory formation at the end of a game. It is a play few people think or talk about, but as a player it symbolized the reward for hard work and dedication.

I have been retired since 1987, almost 25 years. Yet as an ex-player I can remember plays as if they happened yesterday.

Typically the most memorable plays happen in the biggest games. At the time, the biggest game in which I played was my first playoff game in 1976.

I was in my third year as a Patriot, and the game was in Oakland against the best team in the NFL, the Oakland Raiders. We had a lead late in the fourth quarter. Raiders quarterback Kenny Stabler dropped back to pass. Our nose guard, Sugar Bear Hamilton, looped to his right and had a clear shot at the left-handed Stabler. In an effort to change Stabler's ball flight, Sugar Bear had his hands high. After Stabler released the ball, Hamilton's hand hit Stabler on the helmet.

Certainly, today it would be roughing the quarterback, but back in 1976 the rules were much different. You didn't expect a flag. Referee Ben Dreith threw one anyway and gave the Raiders a first down.

In a play you'll read about in this book, they went on to score the winning touchdown with seconds left on the clock. The next week the Raiders defeated a beat-up Steelers team for the AFC championship. Two weeks later they would beat the Minnesota Vikings in Super Bowl XI to become the world champions.

Obviously, the loss was painful. I often wonder whether, if we had won that game in Oakland, we would have continued to the Super Bowl and become world champions. If so, the history of the New England Patriots would be much different.

In the last decade, the Patriots have won Super Bowls and have been the NFL's team of the decade. With championships come many great and memorable plays. When you reflect on the history of the Patriots, I am sure many individual plays and players will come to your mind. This franchise has seen it all, and this book will bring back a lot of memories. GO PATS!

—Steve Nelson

# Acknowledgments

The most important people to thank, as always, are my wife, Mo, and my son, Seamus. Without Mo's support, tolerance of my insanity (both football-related and general), and indulgence of my ridiculous writing process and the burdens it puts on her, I'd never have finished one book, let alone three. And Seamus did more than help me stay sane this time. Sitting in our living room with me in the hours before dawn watching the same plays over and over, he both kept me company and kept me mindful of the assumptions I shouldn't make about what readers do and don't know. For that alone, Seamus all but deserves coauthor credit.

There are two other people without whom I could never have pulled off this project: Ned Cully and Gino Cappelletti.

No one opened more doors for me during my research process than Ned Cully. When I started working on this book, I had never met Ned, who serves as historian for the Gridiron Club of Greater Boston. But without his generosity of time and information, the resource of his amazing memory, his guidance, his encouragement, and the great lengths to which he went to connect me with sources (and

to get them to help me), I'd have been lost. If nothing else, I came away from the project having acquired a friend. *Go raibh maith agat*, Ned.

Gino Cappelletti, one of the all-time Patriots greats, could not have been more helpful and more generous. Gino spent an absurd amount of time on the phone with me, sharing his memories, his observations, and his advice. It was an honor to get to know Gino, and it did this book a world of good. Many thanks, Gino.

My father, Tom Glennon, didn't tell me what to write or how to write it, but he's all over this book—in the chapters about the Pats of the 1970s and '80s, the teams I watched with him as a kid, and in the way I look at Patriots history and the game of football in general. Thanks, Pop.

A lot of friends shared their Patriots memories and their thoughts with me and helped shape what you'll read here. I owe them all a debt of gratitude. They are: Scott Brodeur, Paul Callahan, Andy Curto, Don Fluckinger, Peter Glennon (my cousin), Colleen Kelly, George Lenker, Nolan Richter, John Sanders, and J. Zyskowski.

Bob Hyldburg, whose gem of a team encyclopedia, *Total Patriots*, was a key research tool, connected me with Ned Cully and offered some great comments on several of the plays I included.

Thanks to Michael Emmerich, Adam Motin, Laine Morreau, and everyone at Triumph for giving me the opportunity to write this book, making the thing look great, and making it look like I know what I'm talking about.

Much thanks to the people who connected me with athletes, coaches, and other sources: Stacey James and Donna Spigarolo with the Patriots, Dave Gaylin with the Denver Broncos, Pete Morris with the Kansas City Chiefs, the College of the Holy Cross Office of Alumni Relations, Ann Andelfinger of the Arizona State University Alumni Association, Bill McLaughlin, Wil Johnson, and Kristen Kuliga.

A special thanks to Steve Nelson, who not only shared his thoughts and memories but contributed a terrific foreword.

And last, but absolutely not least, thanks to all the athletes, coaches, and experts who were so generous with their time, memories, and observations: Brendon Ayanbadejo, Raymond Berry, Jim Bowman, Troy Brown, Butch Byrd, Kevin Faulk, Steve Grogan, Tom Greene, Mike Haynes, Antwan Harris, Mack Herron, Ty Law, Gene Mingo, Jon Morris, Lonie Paxton, Babe Parilli, Johnny Rembert, Gil Santos, Aaron Schatz, Ken Stabler, Jan Stenerud, Benjamin Watson, and Tom Yewcic.

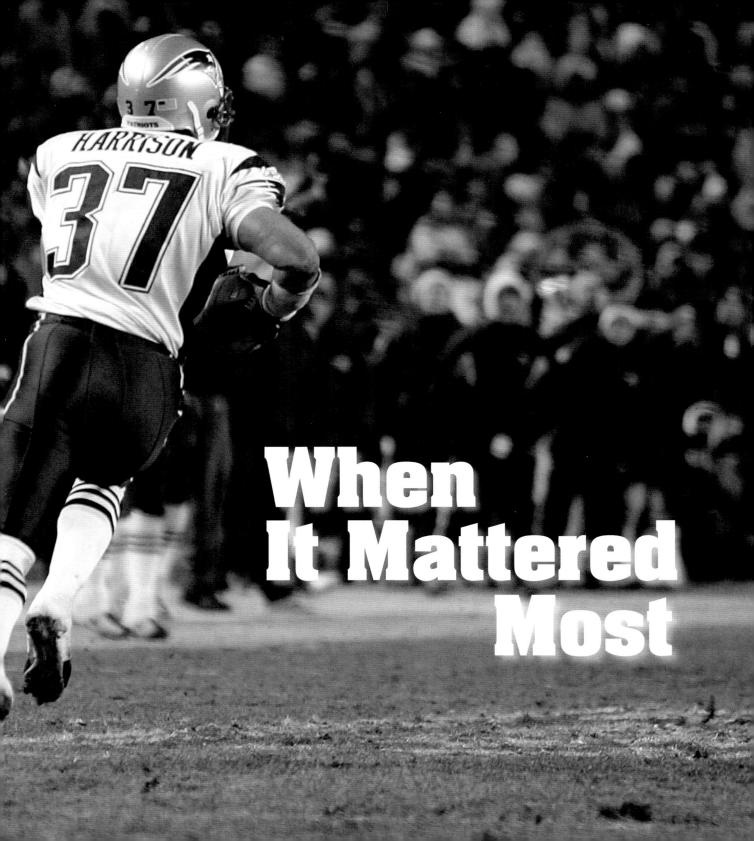

# When It Mattered Most

January 19, 2002

# The Kick

Adam Vinatieri's Impossible 45-Yard Field Goal Changes Everything Forever

The greatest kick Adam Vinatieri ever made—probably the greatest kick *anyone* ever made—didn't come at the end of a Super Bowl. In fact, it didn't come at the end of any game.

It came at the end of an era, the one in which you could always count on things finding a way to go wrong for the Patriots, no matter how good the team might be and how hard the players might work to change the franchise's fortunes.

Vinatieri's 45-yard boot through the driving snow in Foxborough to tie the 2001 Patriots with the visiting Oakland Raiders marked a radical change in direction. The moment was miraculous not only for the fact that the kick connected under nearly impossible conditions, but for the very fact that the Patriots were ever in a position to attempt to tie the Raiders with the clock ticking down in regulation. It was miraculous because it happened to the Patriots—a team that for 42 years had always come out on the wrong end of the biggest moments in the biggest games.

From the AFL's first-ever game—lost by the heavily favored Pats to the Denver Broncos—to the 1964 regular-season finale that was supposed to propel the Patriots to an AFL championship rematch with San Diego but ended up sending Buffalo to the title game, robbery in Oakland in 1976, spontaneous internal combustion in 1978, the right stuff at the wrong time in 1985, and betrayal by the head coach in 1996, the breaks had always managed to beat the boys.

And as the divisional-round playoff game against Oakland moved toward a close, it appeared the Patriots were looking at more of the same. It appeared, in fact, that the Raiders were going to bring the Patriots back down to frozen earth.

The mere fact that the Patriots were hosting a second-round playoff game reflected the degree to which the team had outperformed expectations. The Pats had lost their franchise quarterback, Drew Bledsoe, in Week 2 of the regular season when a cheap hit by New York Jets linebacker Mo Lewis caused an internal injury that threatened the quarterback's life. They'd fallen to 1–3 behind backup QB Tom Brady only to rebound and, winning the final six games of the season, finish 11–5. They took the AFC East title and captured the conference two-seed.

Adam Vinatieri launches the greatest kick in Patriots history, a 45-yard field goal to tie a playoff game against the Oakland Raiders. *Photo courtesy of AP Images.*

# Bound for Canton?

Kickers, as a rule, don't have an easy time getting into the Pro Football Hall of Fame. Jan Stenerud, who enjoyed a 19-year career kicking for the Chiefs, Packers, and Vikings, is the only pure place-kicker ever enshrined in Canton. (Though George Blanda and Lou Groza both made the Hall of Fame, both made significant contributions at other positions.) There's no reason to believe Adam Vinatieri won't someday join Stenerud in the Hall. As Stenerud sees it, stacking the fact that Vinatieri kicked winning field goals with time expiring in two Super Bowls—XXXVI and XXXVIII—on top of a career replete with successful clutch kicks should be enough to do the trick. "Do I expect him to join me in the Hall of Fame?" Stenerud says. "Absolutely I do. He has had two of the biggest kicks ever in professional football and a tremendous career. I hope that he will be there, and I think he deserves it." Aaron Schatz of Football Outsiders takes a more pragmatic route to the same conclusion. "There's a difference between being the best and being in the Hall of Fame," Schatz says. "Adam Vinatieri doesn't have the best kicking percentage of all time—it's very good, it's just not the best—or even the best clutch kicking percentage. He's had more opportunities for clutch kicks than any other player because of the teams he's played for. But once you retire, all that matters is what you did. And what he did was he made all of those kicks."

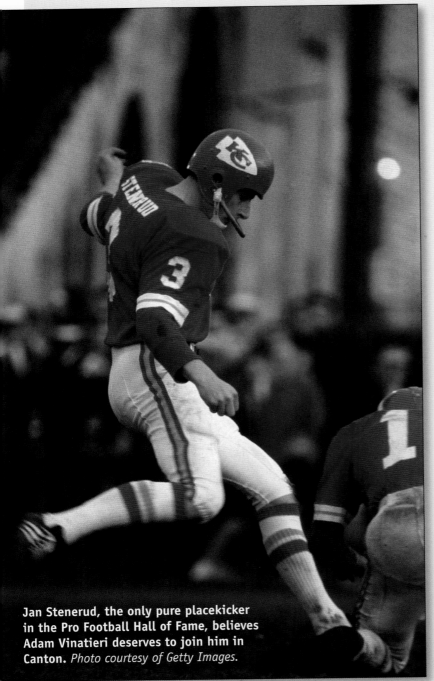

Jan Stenerud, the only pure placekicker in the Pro Football Hall of Fame, believes Adam Vinatieri deserves to join him in Canton. *Photo courtesy of Getty Images.*

The Raiders, though they'd stumbled into the play-offs after starting the season hot, had handled the Jets fairly easily in the wild-card round. And while both teams' offenses had struggled playing through heavy snow that covered the field at Foxboro Stadium and continued to fall hard, creating near-whiteout conditions at times, Oakland entered the fourth quarter with a 13–3 lead.

The Patriots fought back with a solid touchdown drive midway through the period. And they saw their hopes kept alive just inside the two-minute mark, when what initially appeared to be a Brady fumble recovered by the Raiders was ruled an incomplete pass.

But the Pats hadn't managed to make much of their second chance. They stalled at the Oakland 28, where they faced fourth-and-nine with 32 seconds to play. And they sent out the field-goal team to try a desperation kick that would have been tough in optimal conditions.

As Aaron Schatz of Football Outsiders points out, "I don't know how much snow makes a difference, but I know field-goal percentage goes down in cold weather. That's just a fact."

It's also a fact that it was hard to see 10 yards away in the snow that night. And that Vinatieri had to kick from atop four inches of packed snow. And, according to long-snapper Lonie Paxton, officials placed the ball lace-side down at the line, requiring Paxton to snap accurately and Vinatieri to kick accurately despite the laces being packed with snow, a factor that can throw off trajectory.

Still, Paxton delivered the ball, holder Ken Walter planted it securely atop the glacier, and Vinatieri found his footing and delivered.

The ball came out low, rose up just above the level of the crossbar, seemed for all the world to hover in the frigid air—as if it somehow knew a turning point was at hand and wanted to force everyone to recognize the weight of the moment—and carried through the uprights.

The Pats won the toss in overtime and, after a drive that lasted eight and half minutes of game time, Vinatieri booted an academic 23-yarder to win the game and advance the Patriots along the path to Super Bowl XXXVI.

There was no knowing for sure that night how significantly the stars were realigning for the Patriots, but it was clear at least one thing had changed. The big moments in the big games really could go New England's way. Finally.

# Game Details

**New England Patriots 16 • Oakland Raiders 13**

| Patriots | 0 | 0 | 3 | 10 | 3 | **16** |
|---|---|---|---|---|---|---|
| Raiders | 0 | 7 | 6 | 0 | 0 | **13** |

**Date:** January 19, 2002

**Team Records:** Patriots 12–5; Raiders 11–7

**Scoring Plays:**

OAK Jett 13-yard pass from Gannon (Janikowski PAT)

NE Vinatieri 23-yard FG

OAK Janikowski 38-yard FG

OAK Janikowski 45-yard FG

NE Brady 6-yard run (Vinatieri PAT)

NE Vinatieri 45-yard FG

NE Vinatieri 23-yard FG

February 3, 2002

# Setting Up Adam

Brady-to-Brown Brings the Pats into Range for a Super Bowl
XXXVI Win

Super Bowl XXXVI didn't end just with a kick.

Yes, there was a kick. One that made history, that launched a dynasty, and that profoundly altered the legacy of two franchises.

It was a hell of a thing.

But there was a lot more than that. There was also a drive to set up that kick. A drive that forced the entire football-watching world to sit up and take notice of the young quarterback who directed it. And there was a key play by a savvy receiver who made the whole thing count.

If you've lost track of that fact, it's time to go back to the tape. Because it's stunning now just as surely as it was stunning on February 3, 2002.

Of course, back then the mere fact that the Patriots had the ball and a chance to win at the end of regulation was a bit of a poser.

It certainly wasn't supposed to go that way. The St. Louis Rams were supposed to roll the Patriots and capture their second Lombardi Trophy in three seasons. The Rams, after all, were an offensive powerhouse, anointed as all-but-certain champions before the preseason began.

The Rams put up 503 points during the regular season. One of the teams they beat en route to a 14–2 record was New England, a squad that at least appeared at that point to be struggling to find its way.

The Pats were in their second year under head coach Bill Belichick. They'd finished 2000 with a record of 5–11, and in the off-season they'd seen a radical remaking of the roster. Nearly a third of the 2001 team was made up of newcomers, many of them castoffs from other franchises.

Then in Week 2, the team had been forced to make an even bigger change. Franchise quarterback Drew Bledsoe—who'd signed a record 10-year, $103 million contract in the off-season—took a sideline hit from linebacker Mo Lewis in a game against the New York Jets. The hit partially sheared an artery in Bledsoe's chest, and the quarterback wound up hospitalized after the internal injury dumped nearly four liters of blood into his chest cavity.

Troy Brown's heads-up football proved invaluable to the Patriots in the final minute of Super Bowl XXXVI.
*Photo courtesy of Getty Images.*

Bledsoe was lost for most of the season, replaced by Tom Brady, who had been a sixth-round pick in the 2000 draft.

Brady made a splash in his first start, leading the 0–2 Pats to a 44–13 victory over the heavily favored Indianapolis Colts. Then the team settled into a hot-and-cold pattern. The 24–17 loss to the visiting Rams in Week 10 dropped the Patriots' record to 5–5.

Still, Brady had shown his coach something. He was a smart quarterback with an ability to make accurate throws under incredible pressure. He was also a natural leader. It was decided he would keep the job even after Bledsoe was cleared to play in Week 12.

Brady showed he was worth it, leading the Pats on a six-game winning streak to close the season with an 11–5 record and snag the conference two-seed.

And in the closing 1:21 of the Super Bowl, Brady would prove his value yet again.

Though they led for the better part of the game, the Patriots found themselves in a dangerous situation. The defense had held the Rams in check for the first three quarters of the game, but St. Louis came alive in the fourth, scoring a pair of touchdowns to tie the game at 17.

As the Pats took the ball for what would be the last time in regulation, they knew they needed to play for the win.

Brady got the ball at his 17-yard line and took control. On first down, with Rams pass rushers grabbing at him in the pocket, Brady coolly found running back J.R. Redmond for five yards. He threw to Redmond two more times to get his team to the 41.

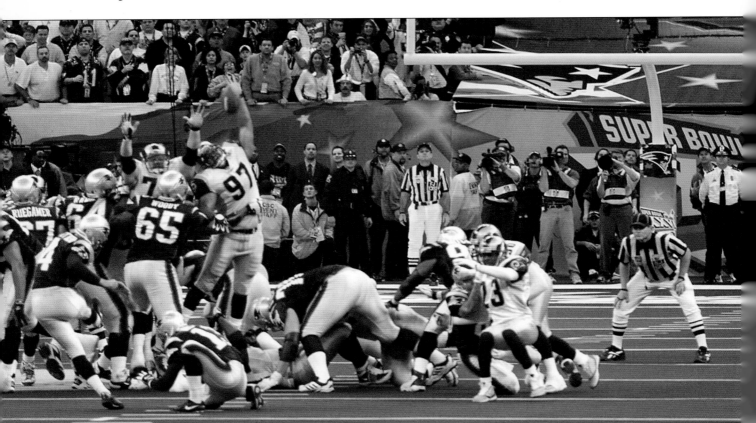

**Adam Vinatieri's Super Bowl–winning field goal sails over the outstretched hand of St. Louis Rams defensive lineman Tyoka Jackson.** *Photo courtesy of AP Images.*

Then, following a first-down incompletion that stopped the clock at 0:29, Brady found Troy Brown for the biggest play of the drive.

Once again facing an intense rush, Brady stepped up in the pocket and hit a wide-open Brown in the middle of the field at the Rams 45. And Brown, rather than looking for extra yardage, worked to save time. Cutting slightly upfield, he made for the sideline, beating a tackler to get there.

The move gave the offense 21 seconds to work with. A six-yard pass play to tight end Jermaine Wiggins got the Pats to the 30, where Brady spiked the ball and set up Adam Vinatieri to make the most important kick in Patriots history: a 48-yard game winner as time expired.

The Patriots were Super Bowl champions for the first time—because of a spectacular kick, a phenomenal drive, and one of the all-time great heads-up plays.

# Game Details

## New England Patriots 20 • St. Louis Rams 17

| | | | | | |
|---|---|---|---|---|---|
| **Patriots** | 0 | 14 | 3 | 3 | **20** |
| **Rams** | 3 | 0 | 0 | 14 | **17** |

**Date:** February 3, 2002

**Team Records:** Patriots 14–5; Rams 16–3

**Scoring Plays:**

STL Wilkins 50-yard FG

NE Law 47-yard INT return (Vinatieri PAT)

NE Patten 8-yard pass from Brady (Vinatieri PAT)

NE Vinatieri 37-yard FG

STL Warner 2-yard run (Wilkins PAT)

STL Proehl 26-yard pass from Warner (Wilkins PAT)

NE Vinatieri 48-yard FG

# Twice as Nice

Gil Santos, who started calling Patriots games in 1972, knows how to put things succinctly: "Adam Vinatieri's kick at the end of Super Bowl XXXVI was the biggest play in Patriots history." It would be hard to argue otherwise. The 48-yarder as time expired wasn't the most difficult or spectacular kick Vinatieri ever made; that distinction goes to the one he booted 45 yards through the driving snow to tie the Oakland Raiders three weeks earlier. But the Super Bowl kick was a thing of beauty. "It was probably as true as you could want," says Gino Cappelletti, who made more than a few big kicks himself during his playing days. "It was a great kick at a great time."

Most important: Vinatieri's first Super Bowl winner turned the hard-luck Patriots, at least for a time, into fortune's favorite franchise. The Pats were one team before the kick passed through the goal posts and another entirely when it got to the other side.

They became a different team yet again two years later when Vinatieri made his second championship kick. The 41-yarder that lifted the Patriots to a 32–29 win over the Carolina Panthers in Super Bowl XXXVIII sparked talk of dynasty (talk confirmed with the team's victory over the Philadelphia Eagles in Super Bowl XXXIX). It also gave Vinatieri a distinction he'll likely enjoy for decades to come. He is the only player ever to post the winning points in the closing seconds of two Super Bowls.

The play Troy made was a huge play. He was in the middle of the field, but he knew he had to get out of bounds. His quick thinking gave Adam enough time to kick the field goal.

—GIL SANTOS

December 7, 2003

# Cue the Snow Fireworks

Tedy Bruschi's Clutch Pick Six Wraps Up a Division Title

Somebody had to do *something* with all that snow. It was everywhere in Gillette Stadium, not least of all piled atop the 28,000-plus empty seats.

Something had to happen with all that energy, too. The fans who had been able to make it to Foxborough through the blizzard had sat through 51 minutes of mostly scoreless football. By the time Tedy Bruschi pulled off the interception and touchdown that effectively sealed a win, fans were beyond ready to pop. And pop they did.

It was almost a miracle that there was anyone in Gillette that evening to celebrate. The snowstorm that had moved into eastern Massachusetts on Friday night hadn't let up until sometime in the second quarter. Over the course of two days, the storm had dumped more than 28 inches of powder over the region. It was everything you could do just to get out of your driveway, let alone find your way to Route 1. Under most circumstances, the Gillette lots would have played host to nothing more than a selection of snowmobiles and maybe the odd dogsled.

Tedy Bruschi heads toward the Dolphins' end zone with an intercepted ball as Rodney Harrison (No. 37) celebrates the victory-sealing play. *Photo courtesy of Getty Images.*

**Tedy Bruschi joins the Gillette Stadium crowd in an impromptu "snow fireworks" celebration of his clutch pick six.** *Photo courtesy of Getty Images.*

But the circumstances at hand weren't in any way run-of-the-mill. The Miami Dolphins were in town, and they were the only thing standing between the Patriots and an AFC East title.

The Pats, who were riding an eight-game winning streak, didn't technically *need* to beat the Fins. The Dolphins were 8–4. And the 10–2 Patriots had beaten them in Miami earlier in the season. A loss would have put New England in a position that might have been uncomfortable but would scarcely have been untenable.

Still, there was the opportunity for the Patriots not only to clinch a division title early, but to keep the heat on Kansas City in the race for the conference's top postseason slot. And that was something the fans, like the team, didn't take lightly.

So 45,000 people risked their lives and their cars to slalom into Foxborough—only to see a matchup in which neither offense could get any kind of traction.

The only score in the first three quarters came at the end of the first. Following a plodding drive in which the Pats spent six minutes and executed 12 plays moving from their own 48-yard line to the Dolphins' 11,

# Snow Telling

Notoriously unpredictable though the weather in New England may be, there's at least one safe bet: If it's after December 1 and you see that the Miami Dolphins are scheduled to visit Foxborough, you'd best make sure you know where your boots are. Snow and the Dolphins just have a way of showing up together.

There was snow still piled on many of the seats in Gillette Stadium in Week 17 of the 2002 season when the Dolphins showed up looking to put the 8–7 Patriots away and wrap up an AFC East title. And when the Fins went ahead 24–13 with five minutes to play, it looked to all the world like the day was theirs. But the Patriots stormed back, tied the game with a minute left in regulation, then won on the first possession of OT. The Pats still missed the playoffs, but so did the Fins, who came out on the wrong side of a tiebreaker with the New York Jets.

And, of course, there was the famous Snow Plow Game from the strike-shortened 1982 season. The Pats and Fins slid back and forth across the glaciated Schaefer Stadium field for most of the game. Then, late in the fourth, the Patriots got close enough to try a 33-yard field goal, and a plow was called out to clear a spot for the kick. John Smith's field goal was the difference in the 3–0 Pats win. And in the off-season, the use of a plow on the field during NFL games was outlawed.

Adam Vinatieri connected on a 29-yard field goal to make it 3–0.

Vinatieri missed on a 54-yard attempt at the end of the first half. And Miami missed out on its only chance to score when Rodney Harrison strip-sacked Jay Fiedler on a third-down play from the New England 10.

Beyond that, the game offered virtually nothing to get excited about…until a Brooks Barnard punt midway through the fourth pinned the Dolphins back at their 4.

Miami made the mistake of trying to throw out of their end zone on first down. Fiedler targeted Chris Chambers in the flat, but Bruschi made a quick move to snatch the ball, then bolted five yards for what would be the game's only touchdown.

Bruschi fell to his knees in celebration, then turned to the stands to dial in the fans, who responded with a spectacle. Grabbing snow two handfuls at a time, they launched it skyward, punctuating every "Hey" in Gary Glitter's "Rock and Roll Part 2" with a fresh powder volley.

A Ty Law interception later in the quarter and a safety on the last Dolphins possession confirmed the win. The Pats took the division. And everyone went home to have a lot less fun throwing a lot more snow.

> **T**o have the ability to recognize the play, get your head in there, and get the ball, shows the kind of athlete Bruschi was.
>
> —STEVE NELSON

## Game Details

**New England Patriots 12 • Miami Dolphins 0**

| | | | | | |
|---|---|---|---|---|---|
| Patriots | 3 | 0 | 0 | 9 | **12** |
| Dolphins | 0 | 0 | 0 | 0 | **0** |

**Date:** December 7, 2003

**Team Records:** Patriots 11–2; Dolphins 8–5

**Scoring Plays:**

NE Vinatieri 29-yard FG

NE Bruschi 5-yard INT return (Vinatieri PAT)

NE Safety, Fiedler sacked in end zone by Green, Vrabel

February 1, 2004

# Setting Up Adam Again

Brady-to-Branch Pass Moves the Pats into Position for Another Championship Kick

It was completely different. Right up to the point when it was the same.

For 59 minutes, Super Bowl XXXVIII had exactly two things in common with Super Bowl XXXVI: Both were close games, and both involved the New England Patriots.

But then, with a little more than a minute to play and the score tied, the Patriots offense had the ball and a chance to end the game in regulation.

The need to score wasn't so pressing this time around. Two years earlier, the Pats were a team that couldn't afford to pass up any opportunity. They had held the high-powered St. Louis Rams to 17 points, only to see the Rams seize momentum late. Overtime would have put New England at the mercy of a coin toss.

Against the Carolina Panthers, it was different. The Pats had come into the game as seven-point favorites for good reason. They were the better squad. They would have as good a chance to win in OT as they did in regulation.

Except for one thing: They had the ball in regulation. There was no guarantee they'd get it to start an extra period. Bill Belichick, ever the aggressive play caller, thought it best to pursue the opportunity at hand.

It was a wise choice if only for the fact that there was no predicting what either offense could do on any given drive.

That much was made clear just before halftime. After the longest scoreless stretch in Super Bowl history—27 minutes of football in which it appeared the game would never be anything but a struggle between two elite defenses—the Pats and Panthers put a combined 24 points on the board in three minutes.

The Pats struck first, making the most of good field position created when Mike Vrabel chopped the ball out of Panthers quarterback Jake Delhomme's hand at the Carolina 20. A five-yard touchdown pass from Tom Brady to Deion Branch and a penalty on the ensuing kickoff that pinned the Panthers back at their own 5-yard line made it appear the half would end with the Pats ahead 7–0.

But Carolina, which to that point had negative-eight yards of total offense, came alive and sprinted to the Patriots' end zone in eight plays. The Pats responded by moving 78 yards in six plays to go back on top by seven. And the Panthers closed the half with a big kick return followed by a 21-yard Stephen Davis run to set up a John Kasay field goal.

Just like that.

As if to make things weirder, the teams reverted to their earlier form after the half, punting the ball back and forth through the third quarter.

The Patriots extended their lead to 21–10 with a touchdown at the start of the fourth quarter. But the Panthers fought their way back in. Two touchdowns—the second of them an 85-yard strike from Delhomme to Muhsin Muhammad following an interception of Brady in the Carolina end zone—put the Panthers on top for the first time. The lead wasn't quite what it might have been, however. The Panthers failed on two-point tries after both scores and ended up ahead 22–21.

The Pats had better luck with their two-point try, faking a high snap and giving running back Kevin Faulk the space to blast into the end zone. The defense couldn't shut the Panthers down, however, and Carolina tied the game at 29 with 1:08 to play.

And so it again came down to Brady and the offense trying to move into field-goal range as the game clock ticked down.

The Pats caught a break when Kasay's kickoff carried out of bounds and the ball was spotted at the New England 40. They moved quickly into Carolina territory but were pushed back across midfield by an offensive pass-interference call.

Two quick pass plays advanced the Patriots to the Carolina 40, but only 14 seconds remained. They needed to make something happen then, or they'd have to take their chances in overtime.

On third-and-three, Brady, ice in his eyes, took the snap out of the shotgun,

Deion Branch's 10 catches for 143 yards were a key factor in the Patriots' victory over the Carolina Panthers in Super Bowl XXXVIII. *Photo courtesy of Getty Images.*

Tom Brady was named Super Bowl MVP for the second time as a result of throwing 32 completions for 354 yards and three touchdowns. *Photo courtesy of Getty Images.*

# The Other Troy Brown: Kevin Faulk

If Troy Brown had been a running back, he would have been Kevin Faulk. Seriously. At times the similarity between the two players borders on uncanny. It starts with attitude: Faulk, like Brown, is the definition of a blue-collar athlete. He works hard and does whatever his team asks. He's been doing it for 11 years, all with the Patriots, and if he's ever complained that he doesn't get enough recognition, he hasn't done it publicly.

But the fact is, Faulk *doesn't* get enough recognition. He's been a consistent contributor on offense, both running the ball and providing a reliable target for Tom Brady in short passing situations. His 418 catches are the most by a running back in Patriots history. He's returned punts and kicks, sometimes with spectacular results. And like Brown, he's been there to strip intercepted balls away from defensive backs. In 2007 he got one back from Baltimore Ravens safety Ed Reed, allowing the Patriots to come out ahead in their toughest match of the season.

In Super Bowl XXXVIII, Faulk had a key two-point conversion, taking a direct snap and rocketing through the one gap. It was Faulk's only score that year (though he'd racked up 1,351 all-purpose yards), but it was critical. Had the two-point try failed, the Pats might have been driving to tie late rather than to win.

And how does Faulk feel about being compared with Brown? "Troy's my idol," he says. "When I came here, I tried to model myself after him." Mission accomplished.

---

dropped back to the 48, and threw a strike to Branch, who was running for the right sideline.

Branch was hit hard by safety Mike Minter before he could get out of bounds. But it didn't matter. Brady and Branch had done what needed doing. They had advanced the ball to the 23-yard line. And the Patriots had a timeout left.

From 41 yards out, Adam Vinatieri showed why they call him Mr. Automatic, drilling his second Super Bowl–winning field goal. And the Pats were champions for the second time in three years.

It had been completely different. But when it mattered, Brady, Branch, and Vinatieri made sure it was entirely the same.

> **T**o us as a football team, it didn't matter: The time, the game, the season. We were doing what we practiced.
>
> —KEVIN FAULK

## Game Details

### New England Patriots 32 • Carolina Panthers 29

| | | | | | |
|---|---|---|---|---|---|
| **Patriots** | 0 | 14 | 0 | 18 | **32** |
| **Panthers** | 0 | 10 | 0 | 19 | **29** |

**Date:** February 1, 2004

**Team Records:** Patriots 17–2; Panthers 14–6

**Scoring Plays:**

NE Branch 5-yard pass from Brady (Vinatieri PAT)
CAR Smith 39-yard pass from Delhomme (Kasay PAT)
NE Givens 5-yard pass from Brady (Vinatieri PAT)
CAR Kasay 50-yard FG
NE Smith 2-yard run (Vinatieri PAT)
CAR Foster 33-yard run (pass failed)
CAR Muhammad 85-yard pass from Delhomme (pass failed)
NE Vrabel 1-yard pass from Brady (Faulk run)
CAR Proehl 12-yard pass from Delhomme (Kasay PAT)
NE Vinatieri 41-yard FG

Rodney Harrison takes off with an intercepted football as Ben Roethlisberger's intended receiver, Jerame Tuman, looks on from the carpet. *Photo courtesy of Getty Images.*

# The Bigger They Come

Harrison's Second-Quarter Pick Six Spells the End of Roethlisberger and the 16–1 Steelers

This time the Patriots weren't the underdogs. Three years after their upset victory over the Pittsburgh Steelers en route to Super Bowl XXXVI, the Pats were back at Heinz Field for another AFC Championship Game. Only this time Vegas had New England giving three points.

Steelers players refused to come out and say they were bothered by that fact, but it's hard to believe it didn't rankle them at least a little.

How could it not? The Steelers had beaten the Patriots in the regular season, ending New England's 21-game winning streak in a match that wasn't nearly so close as its 34–20 final score.

What's more, the Steelers had logged 15 consecutive wins of their own heading into the title match. Yeah, the defending champion Patriots went 14–2 in the regular season, but the title game was being played in Pittsburgh for a reason: The 15–1 Steelers were the conference's top seed.

The Pats defense was rated second-best in the league. The Steelers' *D* was first. And while the Pats were the more dangerous team offensively, it wasn't by much.

Rookie quarterback Ben Roethlisberger went into the AFC Championship Game hot but threw three interceptions against the Patriots' veteran defense.
*Photo courtesy of AP Images.*

The Steelers' problem was that their greatest strength was their biggest weakness. Ben Roethlisberger had turned in a hugely successful season, good enough, in fact, to win him Rookie of the Year honors. The only trouble was that to be named Rookie of the Year, you had to be a rookie. And first-year quarterbacks are notorious for losing big games in the postseason.

In the divisional round, the Steelers were able to squeak by the New York Jets in spite of a poor performance by the quarterback. But the wild-card Jets weren't the Patriots.

In the championship game, the difference was easy to see. Roethlisberger was picked off by safety Eugene Wilson on his first pass attempt of the game. And he continued to struggle mightily through the first half. His performance,

# Game Details

**New England Patriots 41 • Pittsburgh Steelers 27**

| | | | | | |
|---|---|---|---|---|---|
| **Patriots** | 10 | 14 | 7 | 10 | **41** |
| **Steelers** | 3 | 0 | 14 | 10 | **27** |

**Date:** January 23, 2005

**Team Records:** Patriots 16–2; Steelers 16–2

**Scoring Plays:**

NE Vinatieri 48-yard FG

NE Branch 60-yard pass from Brady (Vinatieri PAT)

PIT Reed 43-yard FG

NE Givens 9-yard pass from Brady (Vinatieri PAT)

NE Harrison 87-yard INT return (Vinatieri PAT)

PIT Bettis 5-yard run (Reed PAT)

NE Dillon 25-yard run (Vinatieri PAT)

PIT Ward 30-yard pass from Roethlisberger (Reed PAT)

PIT Reed 20-yard FG

NE Vinatieri 31-yard FG

NE Branch 23-yard run (Vinatieri PAT)

PIT Burress 7-yard pass from Roethlisberger (Reed PAT)

# All Highlights

There wasn't much the Patriots didn't get right in the 2004–05 AFC Championship Game. The game film plays like an extended Patriots highlight reel.

The big moments started coming early. The Steelers' first set of downs ended in a spectacular interception. It came on third-and-three from the Pittsburgh 32. Ben Roethlisberger took the snap out of the shotgun and fired right to Antwaan Randle El, who was wide open at the 48. But the pass was high. Randle El extended, trying to make a play, but only managed to get his left fingertips on the ball, deflecting it toward Asante Samuel. The cornerback couldn't make the pick, but in attempting it, he kept the ball in the air long enough for safety Eugene Wilson to swoop in and scoop it up.

Wilson had a second pick later in the game, a diving grab near midfield of a ball that Roethlisberger threw over the head of wide receiver Hines Ward.

Running back Corey Dillon made a gorgeous 25-yard touchdown run around the right side of the line, buzzing by safeties Troy Polamalu and Chris Hope on his way to the end zone.

A 60-yard pass from Tom Brady to Deion Branch on a post pattern put the first Patriots touchdown on the board. Branch also accounted for the Patriots' last score of the game, going 23 yards on an end-around to put the Pats ahead 41–20 with two and a half minutes remaining.

in addition to a fumble by Jerome Bettis on fourth-and-one at the Patriots' 39, limited the Steelers' scoring to a single field goal through most of the first half.

Still, with the half edging to a close and the Pats ahead 17–3, it appeared the Steelers might be able to close the gap. Roethlisberger had moved his team to the Patriots' 19-yard line, where they faced second-and-six.

But once again, a rookie mistake cost Roethlisberger and his team.

Intent on executing his play, Roethlisberger zeroed in on his tight end, Jerame Tuman, from the moment of the snap. The quarterback's eyes telegraphed his intentions. And Rodney Harrison, the savvy veteran safety, was there to take advantage.

Harrison saw what was coming, waited for Roethlisberger to put the ball in the air, then broke on it. He made the pick in front of Tuman at the Patriots' 13 and dashed down the left sideline. At the 30, he cut toward midfield to allow Mike Vrabel to throw a block on Roethlisberger, the last Steeler with a chance to stop the

> **I** always get charged up when I see a defensive back make a huge play, because I know what a major effect it can have on a team.
>
> —MIKE HAYNES

return. And from there, Harrison strolled into the end zone.

The half ended with the Patriots ahead 24–3. The Steelers still had a shot to right things, but it seemed fairly evident that they had lost their last real chance to make it a game when Roethlisberger delivered the ball to Harrison.

When all was said and done, a Steelers team that hadn't given up more than 30 points in a game all year and that had allowed a total of 40 over its previous five home games had surrendered 41 to the Patriots. The Pats had earned a chance to defend their title in Super Bowl XXXIX.

February 6, 2005

# Super Rodney

Harrison's Sixth Postseason Interception Ensures Back-to-Back Championships

Rodney Harrison's interception at the Philadelphia 28-yard line didn't really win Super Bowl XXXIX. Not the way Adam Vinatieri's kicks at the end of Super Bowls XXXVI and XXXVIII won those games.

Harrison didn't put up the winning points. In fact, he didn't so much as attempt to score in a situation where a lot of defensive backs would have. He simply plucked an errant pass out of the air, ran as much time as he could off the game clock, then went down and let the offense take a final snap and a knee to end things.

But the pick—Harrison's second in the league championship game, fourth in the 2004–05 playoffs, and sixth overall in his postseason career—was the play that sealed the Patriots' victory. And the moment when Donovan McNabb's pass dropped into Harrison's hands was the moment when the New England Patriots went from being the best team of the early decade to being an indisputable dynasty, a franchise worthy of being heralded

along with the Pittsburgh Steelers of the 1970s, San Francisco 49ers of the '80s, and Dallas Cowboys of the '90s as the greatest of the NFL's modern era.

Harrison wasn't the MVP of Super Bowl XXXIX—that honor went to wide receiver Deion Branch, who hauled in 11 catches for 133 yards—but there's little question that the Patriots would not have won without him.

He was a force throughout the game, recording seven tackles and a sack in addition to his pair of picks. His efforts elevated the play of the entire New England secondary, making a mockery of Philadelphia wide receiver Freddie Mitchell's claims that the Patriots' defensive backs weren't worth worrying about.

Harrison was part of two key plays that kept the Eagles off the board at the end of the first quarter.

He showed incredible hustle in picking off McNabb at the Patriots' 4-yard line. Lined up in the middle of the field as the Eagles attempted second-and-goal from the 19, Harrison read

Rodney Harrison's first-quarter interception of Donovan McNabb set up a spectacular Super Bowl performance that would include a second clutch pick at the end of the game.
*Photo courtesy of AP Images.*

McNabb's eyes, saw that he was targeting running back Brian Westbrook near the left sideline, and cut over along the goal line, arriving just in time to get in front of Westbrook and snatch the ball.

Harrison was banged up on the play, but he was back in the game on the Eagles' next possession. On back-to-back plays, he sacked McNabb at the Patriots' 46, then held up tight end L.J. Smith long enough for cornerback Randall Gay to punch the ball out of his hands.

And at the end of a hard-fought match, Harrison made the pick that sewed up a victory for his team.

Trailing 24–21, the Eagles had been given one last chance with 46 seconds left to play. A perfectly placed Josh Miller punt had forced Philadelphia to start their desperation drive at their own 4, and a pair of pass plays had netted them a single yard.

With time winding down, McNabb took a snap out of the shotgun at the 1, backpedaled into the end zone, and

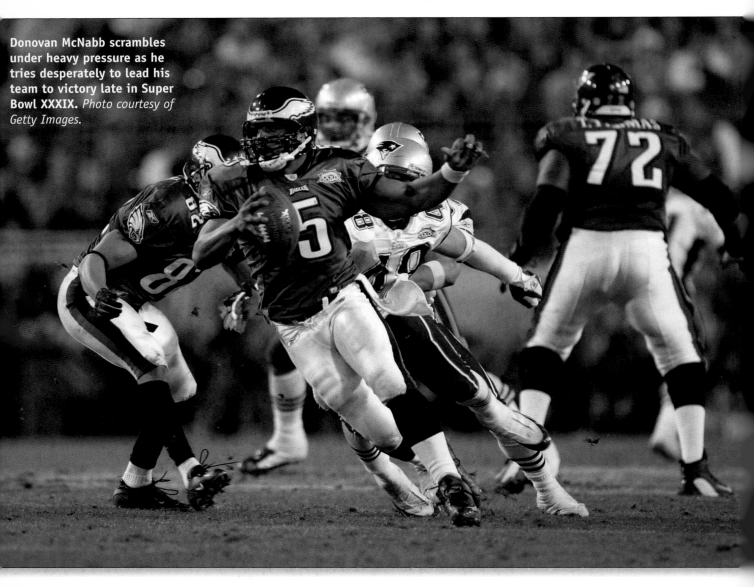

Donovan McNabb scrambles under heavy pressure as he tries desperately to lead his team to victory late in Super Bowl XXXIX. *Photo courtesy of Getty Images.*

# The Three Amigos' Last Stand

The end of Super Bowl XXXIX was a glorious moment in Patriots history. A franchise plagued by bad decisions and bad luck over much of its first 40 seasons had won the NFL championship three times in four short years. A Super Bowl three-peat was unlikely. No team had ever managed it. The realities of a single-elimination playoff system, a draft and free-agency system designed to promote parity, and the physical toll back-to-back 19-game seasons exact on a football team make it hard to imagine that any franchise could possibly pull off that level of dominance. Still, there were few reasons to fear for the team's future success. Few, that is, except for the impending loss of the offensive and defensive coordinators who had been at Bill Belichick's side throughout all four championship seasons. Offensive coordinator Charlie Weis was headed to college, having already accepted the job of head coach at Notre Dame, his alma mater. And it was well known that the Cleveland Browns were only waiting for the Super Bowl to end before offering their head-coaching post to defensive coordinator Romeo Crennel. The brain trust that had built and guided those championship teams was breaking up. And as Belichick, Weis, and Crennel shared an oversized group hug in celebration of the victory, it was clear that the road ahead of the Pats wouldn't be nearly so smooth as the one behind them.

looked left for his tight end, Smith. The pass sailed high. Smith extended but only managed to put his fingertips on the ball, which dropped into Harrison's hands off the deflection.

Harrison recognized that the best move he could make was to kill the clock, which he did. And then, with the play finished, he raised the ball over his head and cut upfield for a victory lap. The Patriots were repeat champions. No team in the modern era has ever managed anything greater than that.

> **C**hances are the Patriots were winning that game whether Rodney made that interception or not. But as we all know, all it takes is one lucky break. He made the right play at the right moment.
>
> —GIL SANTOS

## Game Details

**New England Patriots 24 • Philadelphia Eagles 21**

| | | | | | |
|---|---|---|---|---|---|
| **Patriots** | 0 | 7 | 7 | 10 | **24** |
| **Eagles** | 0 | 7 | 7 | 7 | **21** |

**Date:** February 6, 2005
**Team Records:** Patriots 17–2; Eagles 15–4
**Scoring Plays:**
PHI Smith 6-yard pass from McNabb (Akers PAT)
NE Givens 4-yard pass from Brady (Vinatieri PAT)
NE Vrabel 2-yard pass from Brady (Vinatieri PAT)
PHI Westbrook 10-yard pass from McNabb (Akers PAT)
NE Dillon 2-yard run (Vinatieri PAT)
NE Vinatieri 22-yard FG
PHI Lewis 30-yard pass from McNabb (Akers PAT)

Troy Brown reaches in to make his game-saving strip of Marlon McCree, who has failed to protect the ball.
*Photo courtesy of Getty Images.*

January 14, 2007

# No You Don't

Troy Brown's Instant Changeover from Receiver to DB Saves a Win

If you set out to count the number of games during Troy Brown's 15-year career that the Patriots probably couldn't have won without him, you'll run out of energy well before you run out of games to examine. That's just how it is.

Troy Brown probably won't ever find a spot in Canton. And he was never a household name during his playing days. Not outside New England, anyhow. But Pats fans know without question that Brown was one of the all-time greatest Patriots players. They also know that there was at least one major game in which Brown wasn't simply a significant factor in a Patriots win, he was *the only reason* the team came out ahead.

Without the stunning heads-up play Brown made to strip an intercepted ball from San Diego Chargers safety Marlon McCree in the divisional round of the 2006–07 playoffs, the Pats playoffs run would, without question, have ended a week earlier than it did. The play remains one of the most exciting in Patriots history.

The Chargers weren't just favored to beat the Patriots in their divisional-round meeting, they were the safe money to win Super Bowl XLI. San Diego had finished the regular season with an NFL-best record of 14–2. They were the top-seeded team in the AFC. Their offense, which included league MVP LaDainian Tomlinson, was the most productive in football. Their defense included nine Pro Bowlers. They had outscored opponents during the regular season by nearly 12 points a game.

And while the Patriots, who went 12–4 during the season, had manhandled the New York Jets in the wild-card round, the Chargers were coming off a bye and were at home, where they hadn't lost all season. All San Diego needed to do was play their usual high-powered, hard-hitting brand of football and they were all but assured of hosting the Indianapolis Colts in the conference championship.

The Chargers played exactly the way they were supposed to. On offense, they ran the ball

**Reche Caldwell (No. 87) and Benjamin Watson (No. 84) celebrate the Patriots' unlikely win over San Diego. Also pictured is Mike Wright (No. 99).** *Photo courtesy of Getty Images.*

down the Patriots' throats. And on *D*, their potent pass rush harassed Tom Brady, sacking him twice and forcing bad decisions that led to interceptions.

With 6:25 remaining, the Patriots, who were trailing 21–13, faced fourth-and-five at the Chargers' 41. They had to go for it.

Brady dropped back to pass and, with linebacker Donnie Edwards coming on hard, targeted Reche Caldwell, who was open at the 30. But McCree made a great read, cut in front of the receiver, and grabbed the ball.

The journeyman safety's first mistake was understandable. Rather than slap the ball to the ground, allowing his offense to take over on downs at the 41, he made the pick. That was just a matter of instinct. McCree's second mistake was fatal. Instead of going down and giving the offense a chance to run off most

# The End: An Error?

Things got ugly in San Diego pretty quickly after the Patriots' surprise victory over the top-seeded Chargers. And not just by way of running back LaDainian Tomlinson carping about the Pats' midfield victory celebration. "They showed absolutely no class," Tomlinson said in his postgame media session, "and maybe it comes from their head coach." Tomlinson's frustration was understandable even if the crybaby act was a bit much. The league MVP had gained 187 yards that day rushing and receiving and scored two touchdowns. Under the circumstances, he might well have anticipated a win. And Tomlinson's reaction, as it turned out, was mild compared to that of the team. A month after the loss, the Chargers fired head coach Marty Schottenheimer. The move shocked no one. Schottenheimer had been locked in a feud with general manager A.J. Smith. The playoff loss—Schottenheimer's 13th overall and sixth straight, his second as Chargers coach—provided Smith with an excuse to make a change. Still, the wisdom of firing a coach coming off a 14–2 season was questionable then, and in the post-Schottenheimer era, the Chargers still haven't ended a season with a win. In three seasons under Norv Turner, they're 3–3 in the playoffs and haven't landed in the Super Bowl. Meanwhile, Schottenheimer, who spent six seasons as a player (the final two of them with the Patriots) and 21 as a head coach, has transitioned to broadcasting, working for ESPN and Sirius NFL Radio.

of the remaining time, he looked for a hero's path to the end zone.

Brown, who had spent time filling in for injured defensive backs during the season, seized the moment. He snuck in behind McCree and stripped the ball. Caldwell was there to recover.

The Patriots got a new set of downs and moved quickly to score the touchdown and the two-point conversion that tied the game. And with a little more than a minute to play, Stephen Gostkowski recorded a field goal to win it.

The Pats were probably luckier that day than they were good. But with players like Troy Brown on hand, a team can sometimes make its own luck.

> **B**y our numbers the Chargers *destroyed* the Pats in that game. It never should have been close, let alone the Pats winning the thing, and the biggest reason they did was that strip.
> —AARON SCHATZ, FOOTBALL OUTSIDERS

## Game Details

### New England Patriots 24 • San Diego Chargers 21

| | | | | | |
|---|---|---|---|---|---|
| **Patriots** | 3 | 7 | 3 | 11 | **24** |
| **Chargers** | 0 | 14 | 0 | 7 | **21** |

**Date:** January 14, 2007

**Team Records:** Patriots 14–4; Chargers 14–3

**Scoring Plays:**

NE Gostkowski 50-yard FG

SD Tomlinson 2-yard run (Kaeding PAT)

SD Turner 6-yard run (Kaeding PAT)

NE Gaffney 6-yard pass from Brady (Gostkowski PAT)

NE Gostkowski 34-yard FG

SD Tomlinson 3-yard run (Kaeding PAT)

NE Caldwell 4-yard pass from Brady (Faulk run)

NE Gostkowski 31-yard FG

# On the Offensive

December 4, 1966

# Get Real

### Jim Nance Lands on the Cover of *Sports Illustrated* and Makes the Pats Legit

There are a lot of reasons why fans who got to see Jim Nance play football still talk about him reverently—and that longtime Pats fans were elated to see Nance finally named to the team's Hall of Fame in 2009.

Nance was a marvel to watch play football. He was gigantic for a running back of his era, standing 6'1" and weighing in at more than 235 pounds. A heavyweight champion wrestler as well as a record-setting football player at Syracuse, he not only had amazing strength but knew exactly how to use it. He rarely so much as tried to avoid a tackler. Why bother when it was so much easier just to bulldoze his way through—or more likely, over—them?

Nance's 1,458-yard rushing total in 1966 was the highest recorded by any running back in the AFL's 10-year history. It's only been surpassed by Patriots players twice in the following 43 seasons.

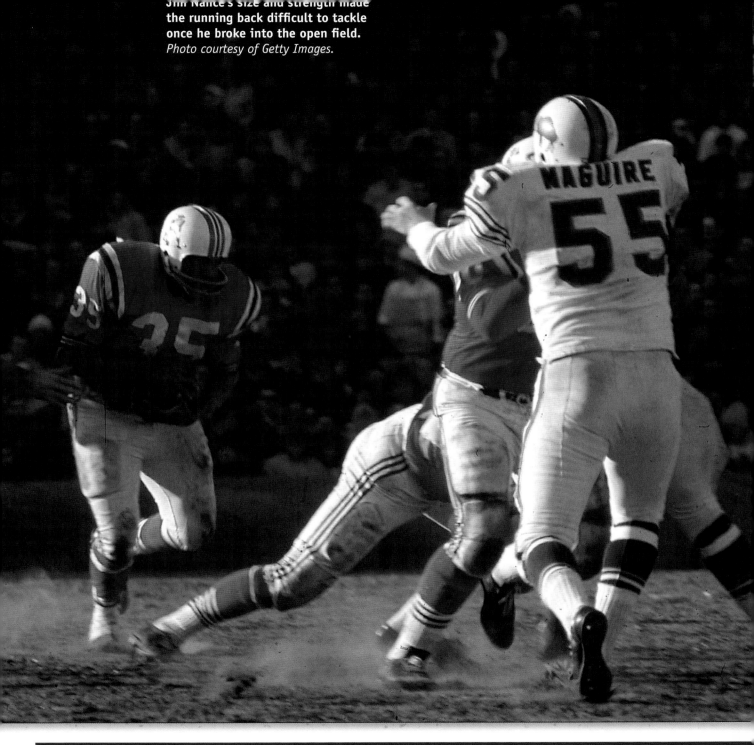

Jim Nance's size and strength made the running back difficult to tackle once he broke into the open field. *Photo courtesy of Getty Images.*

Mike Holovak stepped in to replace Lou Saban after the Patriots' first season and led the team from 1961 through 1968. *Photo courtesy of AP Images.*

I would tell the other offensive linemen, "Just block the guys up front and get out of the way, because otherwise Nance will run right over you."

—JON MORRIS

more important than setting a record. In a Week 12 match against the Buffalo Bills at Fenway Park, he made a run that earned the seven-year-old team much-needed respect from Boston sports fans.

The play came at the end of the first quarter, just three plays after a Booth Lusteg field goal put the AFL Eastern Division–leading Bills on top 3–0.

Four-yard gains by Nance and halfback Larry Garron to begin a drive had landed the Patriots at their own 35.

Nance, teammate Gino Cappelletti remembers, wasn't doing anything out of the ordinary that afternoon.

"He was going up the middle," Cappelletti says. "He wasn't one to go wide and cut back. He wasn't built for that style of running."

On third-and-two, Nance demonstrated the kind of results his style could produce.

Nance carried the ball through the left side of the line between the guard and tackle, glanced left, saw daylight, and ran for it. He rumbled down the sideline, took advantage of a block by Cappelletti at the Buffalo 40, nearly lost his footing but managed to right himself, picked up another key block by tight end Jim Whalen at the Bills' 15, and barreled into the end zone.

The score put the Patriots ahead 7–3 and put them on track to win the game. And the victory gave them a shot at stealing the division title.

More important, though, the score, which was the second-longest rushing touchdown of the AFL season, landed Nance on the cover of *Sports Illustrated*.

# Big Bad Jim

It took nearly 30 years for a Patriots player to top the single-season rushing yards record Jim Nance set in 1966. In 1995 Curtis Martin—playing in a 16-game season and carrying the ball 368 times to Nance's 299—topped the massive fullback's 1,458-yard mark. Martin, who was indubitably one of of the all-time greats, finished the campaign with 1,487 yards, all of 29 ahead of Nance. Corey Dillon made a more convincing show of things in 2004 when he gained 1,635 yards on 345 carries over 15 games.

Only one Patriots running back ever came anywhere close to matching Nance's career rushing touchdown mark of 45. Sam Cunningham, in his 10 years with the team, got to 43. Nance set the record in seven seasons.

Nance, who was selected with the sixth pick of the 19th round in the 1965 AFL draft, had an opportunity to play for the Chicago Bears. But he chose to go to

> **J**im Nance was a player who, once he broke the plane of the line of scrimmage, was impossible to bring down.
>
> —GINO CAPPELLETTI

Boston, where he helped the Patriots develop an NFL-style ground attack in a notoriously pass-happy league.

Slowed by an ankle injury he suffered in 1968, Nance never regained his youthful level of production. In 1972 he was traded to the Philadelphia Eagles but never played for them. He played a season for the New York Jets, spent two in the World Football League, and left the game in 1975. He died of a cardiac arrhythmia and complications from a stroke in 1992 at age 49. In 2009 he was inducted posthumously into the Patriots Hall of Fame.

## Game Details

### Boston Patriots 14 • Buffalo Bills 3

| | | | | | |
|---|---|---|---|---|---|
| **Patriots** | 7 | 0 | 7 | 0 | **14** |
| **Bills** | 3 | 0 | 0 | 0 | **3** |

**Date:** December 4, 1966

**Team Records:** Patriots 7–3–2; Bills 8–4–1

**Scoring Plays:**

BUF Lusteg 11-yard FG

NE Nance 65-yard run (Cappelletti PAT)

NE Parilli 3-yard run (Cappelletti PAT)

"It was a great moment for our team," says Jon Morris, who played center for the Pats from 1964 to 1974 and later enjoyed a long career as a football broadcaster. "In 1966 the AFL was still struggling, and the Patriots were still struggling. We were the second-most-popular football team in town behind the New York Giants."

Nance's long run and the attention it garnered changed the team's image.

"If we were on the cover of *Sports Illustrated*, we must be a real football team," Morris recalls.

The Pats couldn't take advantage of the opportunity they created in beating Buffalo. They won their next game to tie for the division lead but dropped their final match with the Jets and missed the postseason as a result. Just the same, they were finally on the Boston professional sports map. And that was something.

September 15, 1974

# Thanks, Champs

Mini-Mack Herron Sends a Season-Opening Postcard to Miami

When big victories are hard to come by, you learn to savor the little ones. And by the time 1974 rolled around, big victories, as far as the New England Patriots were concerned, were damned near mythological.

It was, to put it delicately, a frustrating era. The Pats had been the least successful team in the AFL's Eastern Division. And with the AFL-NFL merger in 1970, they'd transitioned to being the least successful team in the AFC East.

To make matters worse, all of the other teams from both divisions had managed at least one league championship.

The Buffalo Bills and Houston Oilers both had been repeat AFL champions. The New York Jets were the first AFL team to win a Super Bowl. The Baltimore Colts not only brought a winning NFL history with them when they came over in the merger, but won the Super Bowl in the first season after realignment. And the Miami Dolphins, a franchise that played its first games in 1966, had been to three Super Bowls and won two of them—back-to-back championships in 1972 and 1973.

The Patriots hadn't played in the postseason since getting blown out by the San Diego Chargers in the 1963 AFL Championship Game. They hadn't completed a season with a winning record since 1966. And while they'd shown some flashes in 1973, their first season under head coach Chuck Fairbanks, a pair of losses at the end of the run dropped their record to 5–9.

There weren't a whole lot of reasons to feel hopeful as the defending champion Dolphins arrived in Foxborough on opening weekend. A Pats offense that ranked 16th among 26 teams a year earlier was set to face a Dolphins *D* that had topped the league two years running.

At 5'5", Mack Herron (No. 42) was dwarfed by teammates and opponents alike. *Photo courtesy of Getty Images.*

## Mini-Mack

Mack Herron was easy to spot in any team picture: At 5'5" and 170 pounds, he was the guy who looked like some kid who managed to sneak into the shot. But Herron, who played college ball for the Kansas State Wildcats, wasn't defined by his size but by his skills. Quick and crafty with good eyes for the field and a good head for the game, he spent three seasons with the Winnipeg Blue Bombers of the Canadian Football League before a pot bust got him chased out of the country. When Chuck Fairbanks found him, Herron was back home in Chicago working in sales. Fairbanks brought Herron to Foxborough in 1973, primarily to return kicks and punts. And the move paid off. In his first season with the Patriots, Herron led the league in return yards and finished second, behind O.J. Simpson, in all-purpose yards. In 1974 Fairbanks moved Herron into the starting lineup at running back, playing him alongside Sam Cunningham. That worked out, too. Herron set an NFL record for all-purpose yards in a season, 2,444, eclipsing a mark set by Gale Sayers in 1966. Herron's record was never broken in a 14-game regular season, and his total remains ninth-best of all time. His body and his playing style conspired to cut his career short, and his post-football life didn't go smoothly—Herron did five years in prison for cocaine possession in 1978—but he's turned things around. Today, he's living in his native Chicago, working to keep kids out of gangs.

> **M**ack gave the Patriots some electrifying stuff because of his ability to find holes and corners. He was a weapon if you could get him in the open field.
>
> —GINO CAPPELLETTI

> **E**very team wants to start the season off right. And with our division being so top-heavy, we were just trying to establish ourselves as a team that could compete.
>
> —MACK HERRON

But sometimes hope comes out of nowhere. For the Patriots on September 15, 1974, hope came in the form of 5'5" running back Mini-Mack Herron, a player every bit as tough and determined as he wasn't tall.

The Pats took the season's opening kickoff from Miami and, led by Jim Plunkett, mounted a drive that moved the ball from their own 25-yard line to the Dolphins' 14. Herron did the rest on a single, phenomenal play.

## Game Details

**New England Patriots 34 • Miami Dolphins 24**

| Patriots | 7 | 17 | 7 | 3 | **34** |
|---|---|---|---|---|---|
| Dolphins | 0 | 10 | 7 | 7 | **24** |

**Date:** September 15, 1974
**Team Records:** Patriots 1–0; Dolphins 0–1
**Scoring Plays:**

NE Herron 14-yard run (Smith PAT)
MIA Csonka 1-yard run (Yepremian PAT)
NE Rucker 13-yard pass from Plunkett (Smith PAT)
NE Smith 21-yard FG
NE Plunkett 5-yard run (Smith PAT)
MIA Yepremian 33-yard FG
NE Cunningham 13-yard run (Smith kick)
MIA Briscoe 13-yard pass from Griese (Yepremian PAT)
MIA Csonka 3-yard run (Yepremian PAT)
NE Smith 26-yard FG

Taking a handoff from Plunkett, Herron darted across the line of scrimmage and was met quickly by Dolphins safety Dick Anderson. Herron drove his shoulder into Anderson, bounced off the tackler, and spun a full 360 to his left, nearly falling over backward. Recovering his footing, he took advantage of a key block by John Hannah on Miami's Jake Scott, zipped away from Curtis Johnson, and raced headlong toward the goal line, where he met defensive back Lloyd Mumphord. Herron launched himself into the right shoulder of Mumphord and rolled off the tackler and into the end zone.

"I was so small that when these guys were hitting me, I was like a Ping-Pong ball," Herron says. "I just kept bouncing off them. I remember that's what Darryl Stingley and George Webster used to tell me: 'Just keep on bouncing, man. Keep on bouncing.'"

Herron bounced the Pats into the lead, and the champs never recovered. New England came out ahead 34–24 in what would be the first of five straight victories to open the season.

The streak amounted to little, as the Pats went on to finish the season 7–7. But in those days you took what victories you could get—and you loved guys like Mack Herron for stepping up and delivering them.

**Jim Plunkett never got a real chance to succeed as a Patriot, but in 1974 he helped the team log a season-opening upset over the defending champion Dolphins.**
*Photo courtesy of Getty Images.*

Drew Bledsoe's powerful arm was a key weapon for the Patriots from 1993 through 2000. *Photo courtesy of Getty Images.*

November 13, 1994

# Drew Can

## Bledsoe's OT Touchdown Pass Caps a Season-Saving Comeback

Drew Bledsoe had a point to make, and he was damned well going to make it.

The safe thing would have been to set up kicker Matt Bahr to win the game. It was overtime. Bledsoe had delivered the Patriots to the Minnesota Vikings' 14-yard line. From there it would have been a 31-yard kick for the win.

But that wasn't the way it was going to go. Bledsoe had thrown the ball 69 times to that point in the game. He'd rallied his team from 20 points down late in the second quarter to get them into overtime. As long as it was the second-year quarterback's decision to make (and it was), the Patriots were dancin' with who brung 'em.

And, yeah, you read that right: Bledsoe had thrown 69 times. He'd completed 44 of his passes. He'd racked up 412 yards through the air, throwing for a pair of touchdowns and zero interceptions. He was, to put it mildly, on a tear.

It was just what the Patriots needed, too.

The Pats were sinking when the Vikings got to Foxborough. They were 3–6 for the season, their second under head coach Bill Parcells. They'd lost four straight to get there and had scored a combined nine points in their two previous outings. When stacked on top of the 5–11 1993 campaign, one had to wonder whether even the great Parcells, with his wonderboy first-overall-draft-pick QB, could turn around the piteous Patriots.

And through the first 29 minutes against the Vikings, there had been no cause to reconsider.

Minnesota quarterback Warren Moon was picking the defense apart. Vikings running back Terry Allen, too, was having his way. And the offense was once again proving unproductive.

Parcells made the decision to let Bledsoe take the reins of the offense. After all, *something* needed to change.

# An Arm for the Ages

Both the 45 completions and 70 pass attempts Drew Bledsoe logged in the game against Minnesota still stand as NFL records. Bledsoe also holds the record for pass attempts in a single season—another milestone set in 1994 when he put the ball in the air 691 times. With his 636 attempts in 1995 and 623 in 1996, Bledsoe owns three of the top 10 single-season pass-attempt totals in league history. He comes in sixth on the list of most completions in a season with his 400 successful pass attempts in 1994.

While Pats fans typically remember Bledsoe as a class act, a guy who played through pain and who, right up to the bitter end, put the needs of his team ahead of his ego, it's easy to forget that he was also a great quarterback. A decade into Tom Brady's tenure with the Patriots, Bledsoe is typically remembered for his mistakes, immobility, and—let's be honest—failure to deliver a championship. He should also be recalled for what he brought to the Patriots.

"Drew Bledsoe had one of the best arms in the NFL for four or five years," says Patriots great Steve Grogan. "He came into the league at a time when the running game was becoming an afterthought; teams were putting the ball in the air time and again. Drew Bledsoe was a perfect quarterback for that style of offense."

Drew Bledsoe, shown here with a fractured finger on his throwing hand, played tough and hard for the Patriots throughout his career in New England. *Photo courtesy of AP Images.*

And it was then that Drew Bledsoe stopped being a young quarterback loaded with apparent potential and became a bona fide NFL superstar.

Facing a 20-point deficit with less than a minute remaining in the first half, Bledsoe gunned his way from the New England 32 to the Minnesota 20. With 15 more seconds, he probably would have scored seven. As it was, Matt Bahr got the Pats on the board with a field goal as time expired. The teams headed to the locker room; Bledsoe had thrown for 73 yards to Moon's 234.

Things changed dramatically on the other side of halftime. Bledsoe came out firing and never slowed down. He threw and threw, and then he threw some more, at one point passing on 34 consecutive plays.

At the end of regulation, he again led a drive deep into Minnesota territory only to stall at the 5-yard line. Bahr put up another three to tie the score.

In OT, Bledsoe wouldn't lean on Bahr.

The Pats won the toss, and Bledsoe led them from their 33 to the Minnesota 14.

On first down, Bledsoe took the snap under center, dropped back to the 22 and, standing on the right hash mark, floated a perfect pass to the left corner of the end zone, where it dropped in over fullback Kevin Turner's shoulder and into his hands.

The comeback was awe-inspiring. And it was only the beginning. The win was the first of seven, which was

# Game Details

## New England Patriots 26 • Minnesota Vikings 20

| Patriots | 0 | 3 | 7 | 10 | 6 | **26** |
|----------|---|---|---|----|---|--------|
| Vikings | 10 | 10 | 0 | 0 | 0 | **20** |

**Date:** November 13, 1994

**Team Records:** Patriots 4–6; Vikings 7–3

**Scoring Plays:**

MIN Allen 2-yard run (Reveiz PAT)

MIN Reveiz 40-yard FG

MIN Ismail 65-yard pass from Moon (Reveiz PAT)

MIN Reveiz 33-yard FG

NE Bahr 38-yard FG

NE Crittenden 31-yard pass from Bledsoe (Bahr PAT)

NE Thompson 5-yard pass from Bledsoe (Bahr PAT)

NE Bahr 23-yard FG

NE Turner 14-yard pass from Bledsoe

enough to get the Pats into the postseason for the first time since 1986. They lost to Cleveland in the wild-card round, but it didn't matter.

Parcells and Bledsoe had delivered. The Patriots once again were legit.

October 14, 2001

# The Kid Can Play

Tom Brady Wins Over the Faithful with a Big Fourth-Quarter Touchdown

Five weeks into the 2001 season every football fan in New England knew Tom Brady's name. But no one knew who the young quarterback was.

It was pretty apparent who he wasn't—for better or for worse. The second-year backup QB, a sixth-round draft pick out of Michigan, wasn't the guy the Patriots had given a then-record contract extension—$103 million over 10 years—in the off-season. Brady was the guy who replaced that guy following a devastating injury in Week 2.

He was also a guy whose first two starts weren't what anyone would have labeled unqualified successes.

Brady had done his part in a 44–13 upset win over the heavily favored Indianapolis Colts in Week 3. But credit for the victory belonged mainly to a tough New England defense that intercepted Peyton Manning three times—twice returning picks for touchdowns—sacked the much-ballyhooed quarterback three times, and forced an Edgerrin James fumble. Brady did an admirable job of not losing the game, but no one could claim he won it.

It was easy, on the other hand, to pin the Patriots' Week 4 loss to the Miami Dolphins on Brady. Starting in a hostile environment for the first time, Brady went 12-for-24 for a paltry 86 yards, took four sacks, and lost two fumbles, one of which Miami defensive end Jason Taylor converted into seven points.

The Patriots had been a 5–11 team in 2000, their first year under head coach Bill Belichick. It wasn't looking a whole lot like Brady was going to help them turn things around in 2001.

The visiting team's quarterback was anything but an unknown commodity. Doug Flutie, the local legend, was in his 17th season of professional football, his first with the San Diego Chargers. A good part of the crowd that showed up at Foxboro Stadium that afternoon was more interested in watching Flutie than the home team's erstwhile second-stringer.

For much of the game, fans got pretty much what they came in expecting. With wide receiver Terry Glenn rejoining the starting lineup after a four-game suspension for using a banned substance, Brady was more effective than he'd been in his first two starts. But Flutie, with a good bit of help from rookie running back LaDainian Tomlinson, was still able to keep his team out in front.

Tom Brady stepped up in a major way against the Chargers, leading a huge comeback from a 10-point fourth-quarter deficit. *Photo courtesy of Getty Images.*

When San Diego running back Derrick Harris turned a fumble by Patriots punter Lee Johnson into seven points to put the Chargers ahead 26–16 in the fourth quarter, a good part of the crowd made for the exits.

The fans who left early missed an awakening.

On the possession following the Harris TD, Brady led his team on a sustained drive, completing five of eight passes for 50 yards. Adam Vinatieri capped the drive with a 23-yard field goal. The New England defense held San Diego on the following possession, and a Troy Brown punt

East Boston native Jermaine Wiggins caught only one pass against the Chargers on October 14, 2001, but it was a huge one. *Photo courtesy of Getty Images.*

# A Fond Farewell

No one was sad to see the end of Foxboro Stadium. Built on the cheap by perpetually cash-strapped Patriots founder Billy Sullivan, the facility was sub-par when it opened in 1971. By the time the building hosted its final regular-season game in Week 15 of the 2001 season, fans were long past ready to say goodbye to the stadium's inadequate restrooms, claustrophobic concourse, and painfully ill-advised aluminum bench seating. Still, with the nearly complete Gillette Stadium (then expected to be called CMGI Field) rising up in the background, the Patriots held a farewell party featuring a lineup of players representing each of Foxboro Stadium's 31 years. It was a sweet gesture. Sort of. But the better show by far was the one that took place on the field. Led by Tom Brady, who had held on to the starting QB job even after Drew Bledsoe was cleared to play again, the Patriots took on the Miami Dolphins in a game that would go a long way to deciding the AFC East title. The Pats came in riding a four-game winning streak that included close, hard-fought victories over the New York Jets and the Buffalo Bills. They extended the run to five, beating the Dolphins 20–13. The match featured a trick play in which Kevin Faulk took a direct snap, feigned a run, then lofted a 23-yard pass to Brady. And when the game was over, the reinvigorated Pats spent 10 minutes on the field greeting fans and celebrating the win.

return to the Pats' 40-yard line gave the offense a chance to drive for the tie.

With two minutes to play, Brady completed five of eight passes, taking his team the full 60 yards to the score. He finished the drive with a three-yard touchdown strike to tight end Jermaine Wiggins, tying the game at 26 and forcing overtime.

Brady again moved the team efficiently in the extra period, setting up Adam Vinatieri's 44-yard kick to give the Patriots a win.

Tom Brady might not have been Tom Brady quite yet, but the Pats and their fans were starting to see who he was. And it looked like it wasn't just some backup.

> The staff had eyeballed Tom, and he knew that he might give them the kind of quarterbacking that they were looking for, that quick-decision kind of player. I don't think they were surprised by what he could do.
>
> —GINO CAPPELLETTI

## Game Details

### New England Patriots 29 • San Diego Chargers 26

| | | | | | | |
|---|---|---|---|---|---|---|
| **Patriots** | 3 | 6 | 7 | 10 | 3 | **29** |
| **Chargers** | 3 | 3 | 7 | 13 | 0 | **26** |

**Date:** October 14, 2001

**Team Records:** Patriots 2–3; Chargers 3–2

**Scoring Plays:**

NE Vinatieri 26-yard FG
SD Richey 21-yard FG
NE Glenn 21-yard pass from Brady (kick failed)
SD Richey 27-yard FG
SD Tomlinson 1-yard run (Richey PAT)
NE Smith 1-yard run (Vinatieri PAT)
SD Heiden 3-yard pass from Flutie (kick failed)
SD Harris 6-yard fumble return (Richey PAT)
NE Vinatieri 23-yard FG
NE Wiggins 3-yard pass from Brady (Vinatieri PAT)
NE Vinatieri 44-yard FG

October 19, 2003

# Taking Control

### Another Huge Brady-to-Brown Pass Puts the Pats in the AFC East Driver's Seat

Pro Player Stadium wasn't ready for the Patriots—with the Florida Marlins in the World Series, the multi-use facility's field was still set up for baseball—but the Miami Dolphins certainly were.

That was nothing new. The Dolphins always seemed to bring a little something extra to the field when the Patriots came to visit. They had beaten New England five times straight in Miami. And they had an added incentive to make it six: payback.

The 2002 Patriots hadn't accomplished much, but they had managed to deny their old rivals a playoff berth. With a Week 17 victory in Foxborough, the Pats put the Dolphins at a tiebreaker disadvantage that allowed the New York Jets to steal the AFC East title.

That was one thing. The 2003 division race was another. The Patriots had done a nice job of overcoming a shaky start, building their record to 4–2. But at 4–1, the Dolphins still held a half-game advantage. And they weren't interested in surrendering it on their own turf. Or the Marlins' diamond. Whatever.

To top things off, the Patriots were continuing to deal with mounting injury problems. In addition to Rosevelt Colvin, who was gone for the season, and Mike Vrabel and Ted Washington, who were continuing to miss

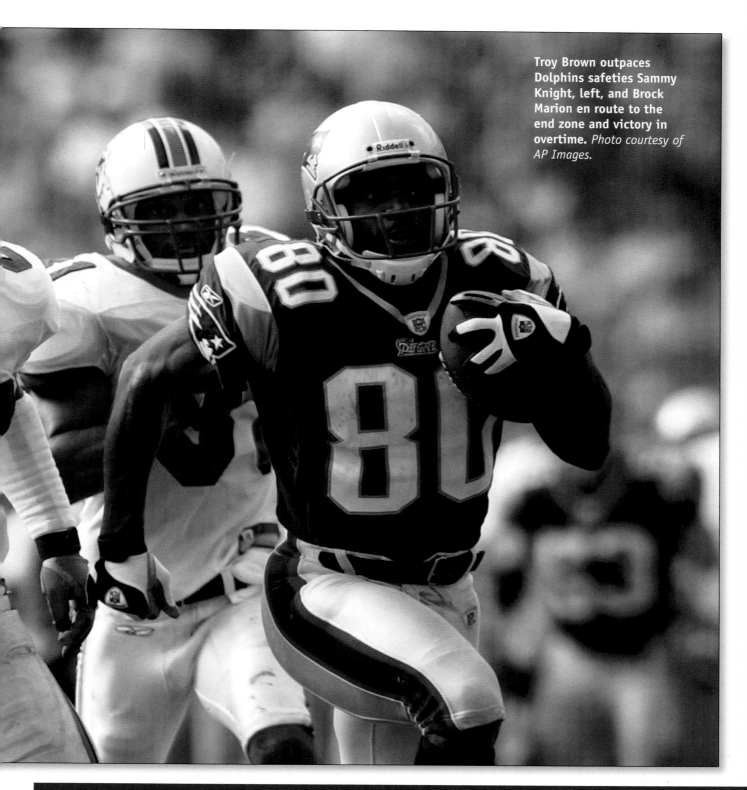

Troy Brown outpaces Dolphins safeties Sammy Knight, left, and Brock Marion en route to the end zone and victory in overtime. *Photo courtesy of AP Images.*

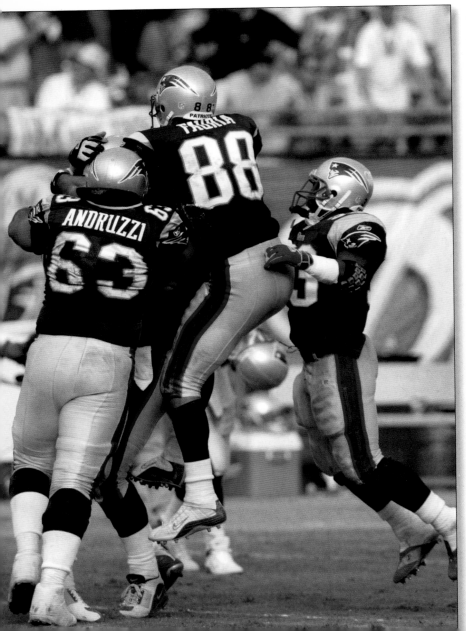

time with broken bones, the Pats were playing without Willie McGinest, Ty Law, and Antowain Smith.

Winning wasn't going to be easy. It seemed like maybe it wasn't even going to be possible.

Then the turnovers started. Dolphins quarterback Jay Fiedler threw a deep pass that was knocked away from wide receiver Derrius Thompson by Asante Samuel and picked off by Eugene Wilson. And wide receiver Chris Chambers fumbled at the Dolphins' 42, setting up an Adam Vinatieri field goal that put up the first points of the game. That offered at least a glimpse of real hope.

But the Pats gave the ball away repeatedly, too.

Through regulation, neither offense had much luck locating the end zone. And when Richard Seymour blocked a 35-yard field goal attempt by Miami's Olindo Mare just after the two-minute warning, it was clear the game was going to overtime.

Not much changed in the extra period.

The Dolphins got the ball first and drove to the Patriots' 17-yard line. But Mare, kicking off the dusty Marlins' base path and concerned about another block, pushed the kick wide.

The Patriots advanced the ball to midfield and then, after nearly losing a fumble, were forced to punt.

Miami took over at their own 30 and moved close to midfield before things fell

**The Patriots' offense celebrates the Brady-to-Brown touchdown pass that gave them control of the AFC East.**
*Photo courtesy of Getty Images.*

# Where Is Brown? There Is Brown.

"If I had to list the top 10 all-around football players—smart, durable, make all the plays, do all the things—Troy Brown would be way up there." That's Gino Cappelletti saying that. And that isn't all. The Patriots Hall of Fame wide receiver/place-kicker, former coach, and longtime radio analyst also has this to say about Brown: "In the '50s and '60s, the team that had more players with greater football instincts was usually the team that won. You had to have guys who knew the game and who could do whatever you called on them to do. Troy Brown could have played in that era. He could have played in any era."

Over his 15 seasons with the Patriots, Brown simply and consistently did whatever his team asked of him. An eighth-round draft pick out of Marshall University, Brown initially found his place with the Patriots returning punts. And he insisted on continuing in that role throughout his career, even

> **T**ough games come down to who makes the plays when it really matters.
>
> —TROY BROWN

as he led the team in receptions during the 2001 campaign. In 2004, as injuries piled up in the Pats' defensive secondary, Brown pulled duties there. Playing nickel back over the final nine games of the season, he logged three interceptions. He continued to play key roles on both sides of the ball in the 2004–05 postseason.

Brown, who retired in 2008, holds team records for receptions (557), postseason receptions (58), punt returns (252), and punt-return yards (2,625).

Troy Brown could do anything. And he did.

apart. On third-and-12 from the Miami 45, Tedy Bruschi shot the one gap and grabbed Fiedler by the jersey. The quarterback narrowly escaped a sack, spinning away from Bruschi. But, still under heavy pressure, Fiedler lofted a pass down the right sideline and into the hands of cornerback Tyrone Poole at the Patriots' 18-yard line.

On the very next play, the Pats went for broke.

Taking the snap from under center, Tom Brady froze the secondary with a pump fake, giving Troy Brown time to get behind safeties Brock Marion and Sammy Knight on a deep route. Brady shifted left and launched a pass down the sideline, hitting Brown in stride at the Dolphins' 35. Brown accelerated slightly to stay ahead of the pursuing DBs, then high-stepped into the end zone.

With the 82-yard strike, the Patriots had come out ahead in yet another tough match. They had taken control of the division. And they would win two Super Bowl championships before ever having reason to so much as think about looking back.

## Game Details

**New England Patriots 19 • Miami Dolphins 13**

| | | | | | | |
|---|---|---|---|---|---|---|
| **Patriots** | 3 | 3 | 7 | 0 | 6 | **19** |
| **Dolphins** | 0 | 10 | 3 | 0 | 0 | **13** |

**Date:** October 19, 2003

**Team Records:** Patriots 5–2; Dolphins 4–2

**Scoring Plays:**

NE Vinatieri 25-yard FG

MIA Chambers 6-yard pass from Fiedler (Mare PAT)

MIA Mare 23-yard FG

NE Vinatieri 30-yard FG

MIA Mare 34-yard FG

NE Givens 24-yard pass from Brady (Vinatieri PAT)

NE Brown 82-yard pass from Brady

Randy Moss outruns James Butler down the sideline on the way to his record 23rd touchdown of the season.
*Photo courtesy of Getty Images.*

December 29, 2007

# Make It a Double

In a Single Play, Brady and Moss Set New NFL Touchdown Records

In time it will start to seem special again, as special as it really was. In a decade maybe. Or a little more than that. When the memory of Super Bowl XLII ceases to burn so hot and you can get close without reliving the pain.

Brady to Moss. Brady to Moss. Brady to Moss. Touchdown pass after touchdown pass, 23 times in a single season. It was a phenomenal thing to watch. And if the whole thing hadn't fallen apart at the end, we'd all still be watching it again and again. On ESPN. On the NFL Network. On DVD. You wouldn't be able to get away from it. You wouldn't want to. And you truly wouldn't care one bit about the fact that it made fans of every other team in the NFL hate the Patriots even more than they already did.

You'd start in Week 1 in New Jersey, watching Moss fly down the field and catch a 51-yard touchdown in stride with three Jets defensive backs around him. You'd hear about how it was one of nine catches Moss made for 183 yards in his Patriots debut. And how the "experts" who said the future Hall of Fame wide receiver was washed up when the Patriots acquired him stopped talking so loud after that.

You'd revisit Week 7 in Miami and watch Brady find Moss for two scores in double coverage, one for 35 yards and another, caught one-handed, for 50.

You'd watch the red-hot quarterback and receiver connect for four touchdowns in the first half against the Buffalo Bills in Week 11.

You'd see them hook up for two TDs in a 34–13 Week 14 blowout of the Pittsburgh Steelers in Foxborough, including a 63-yard bomb with Moss running behind coverage on play action. You'd also marvel in the same game at a double-lateral play in which Moss got the ball back to Brady so the quarterback could hit Jabar Gaffney for a 56-yard score.

Along the way you'd take time to admire the rest of the offense too, especially Wes Welker, who would wow you all over again with his 112 catches for 1,175 yards and eight touchdowns.

You'd pause at Brady's 32nd touchdown pass of the season, a three-yard toss to Welker against the Colts in Indianapolis in Week 9, noting that the score broke Babe Parilli's 43-year-old single-season franchise touchdown record.

When the Week 17 highlights came up, you'd follow the Patriots back to the Meadowlands, this time to face the Giants.

You'd watch Brady hit Moss in double coverage in the right corner of the end zone in the second quarter, knowing the play tied Moss with Jerry Rice for most touchdown catches in a season and tied Brady with

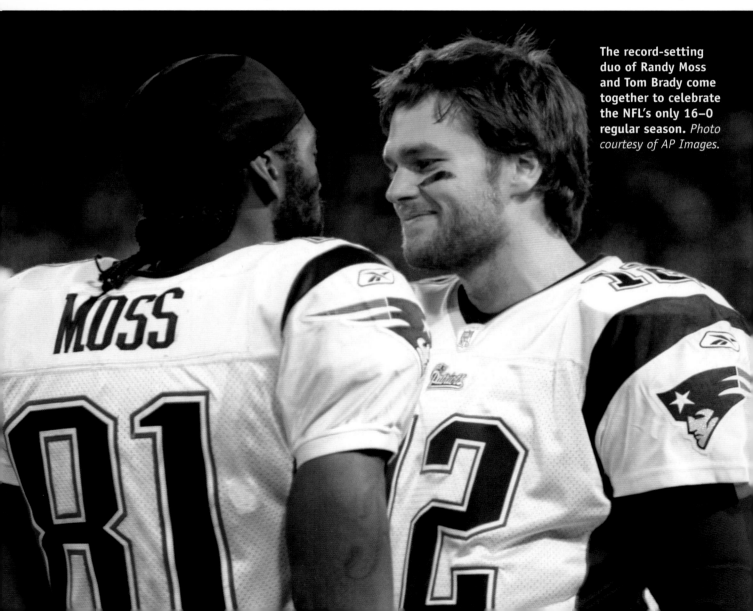

The record-setting duo of Randy Moss and Tom Brady come together to celebrate the NFL's only 16–0 regular season. *Photo courtesy of AP Images.*

Peyton Manning for the most touchdown throws in a season.

And then, early in the fourth quarter, with the Patriots trailing 28–23 and looking for the win to get to 16–0, you'd see Moss beat free safety Gibril Wilson deep down the right sideline on second-and-10 from the Patriots' 35-yard line only to drop Brady's pass. Then you'd watch the Pats run the exact same play again. Only this time, you'd see Moss burn by strong safety James Butler, catch Brady's pass in stride at the 22, and cruise into the end zone.

You'd remember the records: 50 touchdown passes and 23 touchdown catches on one play (and 589 points in a season for the team).

Someday, you'll do it, too. Watch it, and don't think about what comes later. And just enjoy it. And smile.

# Game Details

**New England Patriots 38 • New York Giants 35**

| Patriots | 3 | 13 | 7 | 15 | **38** |
|---|---|---|---|---|---|
| Giants | 7 | 14 | 7 | 7 | **35** |

**Date:** December 29, 2007

**Team Records:** Patriots 16–0; Giants 10–6

**Scoring Plays:**

NYG Jacobs 7-yard pass from Manning (Tynes PAT)

NE Gostkowski 37-yard FG

NE Moss 4-yard pass from Brady (Gostowski PAT)

NYG Hixon 74-yard kickoff return (Tynes PAT)

NE Gostkowski 45-yard FG

NE Gostkowski 37-yard FG

NYG Boss 3-yard pass from Manning (Tynes PAT)

NYG Burress 19-yard pass from Manning (Tynes PAT)

NE Maroney 6-yard run (Gostkowski PAT)

NE Moss 65-yard pass from Brady (Maroney run)

NE Maroney 5-yard run (Gostkowski PAT)

NYG Burress 3-yard pass from Manning (Tynes PAT)

# You Can't Make It Up

Randy Moss came to the New England Patriots on Day 2 of the 2007 NFL Draft. The trade that sent the future Hall of Famer from the Oakland Raiders to the Patriots cost New England a fourth-round pick. That's it. The Raiders, who had sent the Minnesota Vikings a first-rounder and a seventh-rounder, along with linebacker Napoleon Harris, in a deal to acquire Moss just two years earlier, were willing to let him go for a fourth-round selection. Moss hadn't single-handedly turned the flagging franchise around. And the Oakland coaching staff had come to the conclusion that Moss's best days were behind him. They weren't alone. Conventional wisdom around the league held that Moss was washed up. Oakland's asking price was low mainly because there was no one willing to pay anything higher. What's better, the pick New England swapped for Moss wasn't their own. It had come from San Francisco on Day 1 of the draft to sweeten a deal in which the Pats sent the 49ers Seattle's 2007 first-round pick (acquired in exchange for Deion Branch) for the Niners' 2008 first-rounder. (The Pats would ultimately trade down from the eighth spot, which is where San Francisco landed; pick up additional choices; and draft Jerod Mayo, the 2008 AP Defensive Rookie of the Year.) And as if all that weren't more than enough, the Pats also used a second-round pick and a seventh-round pick in 2007 to pry restricted free agent Wes Welker away from the Miami Dolphins. *That* is a successful draft.

**W**hen they traded for Randy Moss, I told Bill Belichick, "That guy's going to lead the league in touchdowns," but I didn't have any idea he would do *that.*

—JON MORRIS

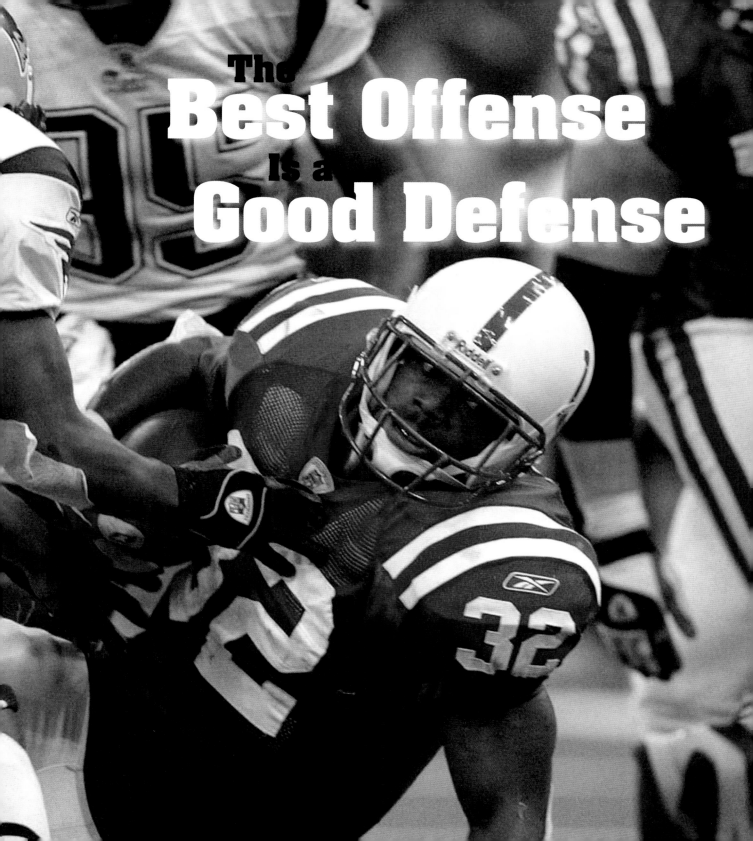

The
**Best Offense**
Is a
**Good Defense**

December 10, 1978

# That's the Stuff

Mike Haynes Pins the Bills Back and Sets Up a Pats Win

Mike Haynes doesn't remember the play. He laughs to think about it.

"Yeah, it sounds like it was pretty big, but I just don't remember it at all," Haynes says.

Fair enough. Haynes is a Hall of Famer. He was one of the best cornerbacks ever to play the game. He earned a Super Bowl ring as a member of the Los Angeles Raiders. Clearly, there were bigger games in his career than the one in which the 1978 Patriots clinched the franchise's first AFC East title.

That's not to mention that Haynes made 46 interceptions in his career, two of which he returned for touchdowns. One of his picks was of Joe Theismann in Super Bowl XVIII, an honest-to–John Facenda career highlight. He also returned 112 punts for 1,168 yards and two TDs.

So Mike Haynes obviously made a few plays he was destined to find more memorable than a tackle—regardless of what that tackle may have meant.

But neither bigger games nor bigger memories account entirely for the fact that Haynes doesn't remember the time he put the Bills in an impossible situation and set up a comeback victory for the Pats.

The truth is that the game is obscured by what came next.

"What I really remember is the locker room in Miami, when they told us the coach was leaving the team," Haynes says.

It makes sense. The split between owner Billy Sullivan and coach Chuck Fairbanks that pulled the rug out from under one of the best Patriots squads ever assembled is what almost everyone remembers from that season. (Or at least about the end of it. The preseason injury that crippled Darryl Stingley also stands out.)

Fairbanks was a brilliant football coach but a difficult personality. Sullivan was a generous and gregarious man and by most accounts a man of good intentions. But his

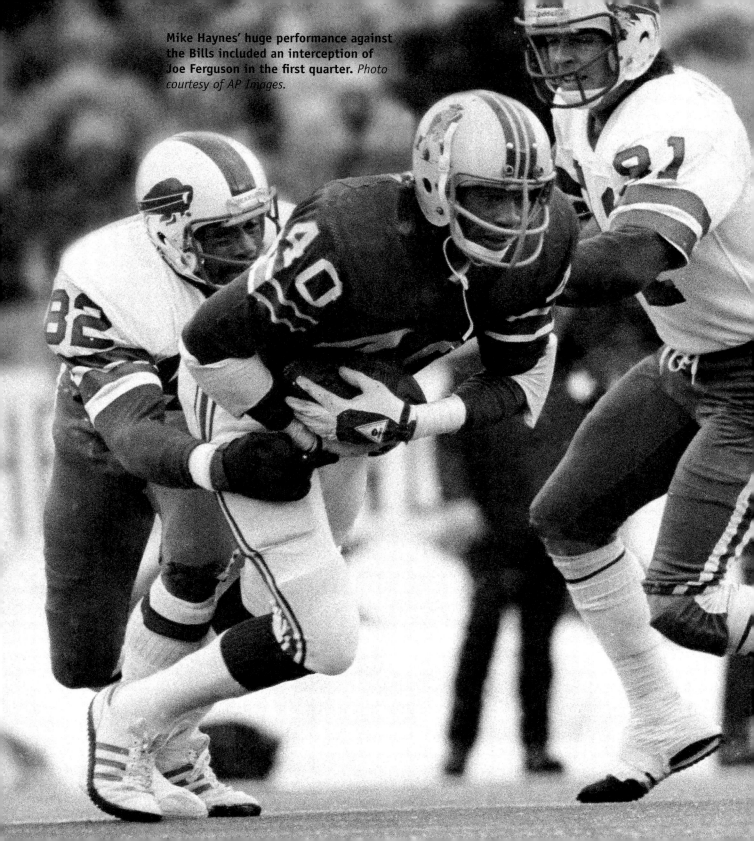

Mike Haynes' huge performance against the Bills included an interception of Joe Ferguson in the first quarter. *Photo courtesy of AP Images.*

# Game Details

**New England Patriots 26 • Buffalo Bills 24**

| | | | | | |
|---|---|---|---|---|---|
| Patriots | 0 | 7 | 7 | 12 | **26** |
| Bills | 0 | 10 | 7 | 7 | **24** |

**Date:** December 10, 1978
**Team Records:** Patriots 11–4; Bills 4–11
**Scoring Plays:**
BUF Hooks 28-yard run (Dempsey PAT)
NE Cunningham 4-yard run (Posey PAT)
BUF Dempsey 26-yard FG
BUF Miller 32-yard run (Dempsey PAT)
NE Grogan 4-yard run (Posey PAT)
NE Ivory 20-yard run (Posey PAT)
BUF Lewis 21-yard pass from Ferguson (Dempsey PAT)
NE Safety, Jackson run out of end zone by Fox
NE Posey 21-yard FG

team's finances were never solid, and that led to problems with both players and coaches.

Fairbanks' growing frustration over six seasons led him to accept a job as head coach at the University of Colorado. He started recruiting while the Patriots were still playing. And when Sullivan found out, he suspended the coach just before the final regular-season game in Miami. Fairbanks was allowed to return for the postseason, but by then the team was in disarray. They were beaten handily in Foxborough by their old AFL Eastern Division rivals, the Houston Oilers.

But before things fell apart, there was that brief, glorious moment at Schaefer Stadium. The Pats, who had entered the game with a chance to win the division, had trailed the 4–10 Bills for most of the afternoon. They saw a chance to go ahead with four minutes remaining disappear as Sam Cunningham lost a fumble at the Buffalo 2-yard line. But the D responded, and Buffalo soon faced third-and-six from their 6.

Running back Terry Miller took the handoff from quarterback Joe Ferguson and cut upfield. But Haynes anticipated the play, stormed in, and caught Miller just short of the sticks.

The stop forced the Bills to punt out of their end zone, and they opted to take a safety rather than risk a block. That got the Pats to within a point. And an efficient drive following the free kick ended with the game-winning field goal by David Posey.

If it hadn't been for the organizational meltdown that followed, the game and the stop that set up the win would probably still be celebrated. Or at least, you know, remembered.

# Split Decision

Mike Haynes is the only player inducted into the Pro Football Hall of Fame as a member of two teams. That's not a special distinction based on how well he played. It's a fluke. The Hall of Fame assigns players to the team with which they spent the greatest number of seasons. (That's right, fans. That means Rodney Harrison would go in as a member of the Chargers and Randy Moss as a Viking.) And Haynes spent exactly seven seasons with both the Patriots and the Raiders. So he's doubled up. It wasn't always the case, but Haynes says he's proud to be recognized for both of his team affiliations. Haynes left the Pats in 1983 as the result of a contract impasse. He didn't have great feelings about the team when he left, but Robert Kraft changed that. "When he bought the team, he took a lot of steps to make me feel good about having been a Patriot," Haynes says. When the Patriots reached Super Bowl XXXVI, Haynes was working as a league executive. He was at the game, but he wasn't supposed to have a rooting interest. Still, he says, he enjoyed seeing New England come away with its first championship. "I felt really proud that I could say I was a Patriot," he recalls. "For a long time, people thought of me as a Raider, and I didn't mind. Now I feel proud about my time on both teams, because I played with some great players."

After leaving the Patriots, Mike Haynes played seven seasons with the Los Angeles Raiders. He's in the Hall of Fame as both a Patriot and a Raider. *Photo courtesy of Getty Images.*

A severe ankle sprain didn't stop Ty Law from playing or from logging a spectacular 65-yard interception return for a touchdown. *Photo courtesy of Getty Images.*

October 5, 2003

# And the Law Won

## Ty's Clutch Pick Six Turns Around a Season and Launches a Winning Streak

Some plays you know are huge as soon as they happen, even if the reasons they're huge aren't immediately apparent.

Ty Law's 65-yard pick six against the Tennessee Titans in Week 5 of 2003 was one of those.

The play capped a hard-fought victory against a tough, physical football team. And the win got the Pats to 3–2 for the season. It was big for that alone.

But the play was more than that.

Law's pick was pivotal in Patriots history. It marked the transformation of a team that struggled through the opening weeks of the season into a juggernaut of historic proportions. The win over the Titans was the first in an NFL-record 21-game streak and the first in a 32–2 run that included back-to-back Super Bowl victories. It was the introduction of the first dynasty of the salary-cap era.

Even before so much as another game played out, however, the victory had significant import.

The 2003 Patriots got off to a shaky start. Five days before opening weekend, the team released veteran safety Lawyer Milloy as the result of a contract dispute, and the move was roundly criticized in the media. ESPN's Tom Jackson famously reported that it had created a rift between Bill Belichick and his players. ("Let me say this clearly: They hate their coach.")

# Way to Pick 'Em

Ty Law's interception against Tennessee was bigger than most fans realize. But Law made much bigger picks during his 10 seasons with the Pats. The biggest, of course, was the 47-yard pick six that put New England's first points on the board in Super Bowl XXXVI. It came early in the second quarter with the St. Louis Rams ahead 3–0. Kurt Warner, under pressure from Mike Vrabel, floated a pass toward Isaac Bruce on an out pattern. Law jumped in front of Bruce, snatched the ball, and zipped into the end zone. "It's hard to describe the feeling of that play," Law says. "We gave everything we had that day, and when you can make a play like that and change the momentum to your side, that's something you never forget." And as if that weren't enough, Law also played a major role in the Patriots' victory over Indianapolis in the 2003–04 AFC Championship Game. Law picked off Peyton Manning three times that day. His first interception of the game, at the New England 35-yard line, set up a second-quarter drive through which the Patriots extended their lead to 13–0. His third, which came midway through the fourth quarter, was made at the Patriots' 11-yard line and returned to the 31. It preserved a 21–7 lead and effectively sealed New England's victory. "I was always on Manning's go-to guy, Marvin Harrison," Law says. "So I knew it was going to be him or me."

> Ty Law deserves a special place in Patriots history. He has been one of the best cornerbacks of his era.
>
> —MIKE HAYNES

The bigger issues, though, were the ones on the field. The Pats opened with a 31–0 loss to the Buffalo Bills. And although they bounced back to beat the Philadelphia Eagles and the New York Jets, a Week 4 loss to the Washington Redskins, in which Tom Brady threw three interceptions, cast new and serious doubt on the team's potential.

Injuries, too, had become a cause for concern. Linebacker Rosevelt Colvin was gone for the season. Mike Vrabel and nose tackle Ted Washington both were nursing broken bones. And Law was doing his best to play through a severe high ankle sprain suffered in the win over the Jets.

The Titans, a physical team that had beaten the Pats convincingly in 2002, weren't the opponents anyone wanted to see.

## Game Details

### New England Patriots 38 • Tennessee Titans 30

| | | | | | |
|---|---|---|---|---|---|
| **Patriots** | 7 | 0 | 14 | 17 | **38** |
| **Titans** | 6 | 7 | 3 | 14 | **30** |

**Date:** October 5, 2003

**Team Records:** Patriots 3–2; Titans 3–2

**Scoring Plays:**

TEN Hentrich 48-yard FG

TEN Anderson 43-yard FG

NE Brown 58-yard pass from Brady (Vinatieri PAT)

TEN McNair 1-yard run (Anderson PAT)

NE Smith 1-yard run (Vinatieri PAT)

TEN Anderson 33-yard FG

NE Cloud 1-yard run (Vinatieri PAT)

TEN Anderson 37-yard FG

NE Vinatieri 48-yard FG

TEN McNair 1-yard run (Calico pass from McNair)

NE Cloud 15-yard run (Vinatieri PAT)

NE Law 65-yard INT return (Vinatieri PAT)

TEN Anderson 41-yard FG

The match was every bit as tough as expected. Both teams played hard, and the scoreboard reflected it. When Patriots running back Mike Cloud found the end zone with 3:14 remaining to play, putting the Pats ahead 31–27, he effected the seventh lead change of the game.

Steve McNair responded to Cloud's TD by moving his team quickly into New England territory.

Law, who had been on the sideline through most of the second half because of his injury, talked his way back into the game. Having seen McNair complete passes of 40 and 45 yards to Tyrone Calico in the half, Law concluded he needed to do something to stop the bleeding.

McNair saw a gimpy corner and decided he could take advantage. On second-and-three from the New England 40, he targeted Calico five yards away. But Law would have none of it. He broke on the ball, picked off the pass, and toughed out a 65-yard return down the sideline to the end zone.

With the extra point, the Pats extended their lead to 11.

The Titans were able to add a field goal with 36 seconds left on the board, but their subsequent on-side kick failed, and the game ended with the Pats ahead 38–30.

No one would have or could have predicted the level of success that was to follow. But it was obvious that things had changed—you could feel it just as soon as Ty Law crossed into the end zone.

**Steve McNair was a great football player, but he underestimated Ty Law and paid a price for it.** *Photo courtesy of Getty Images.*

November 30, 2003

# The Stop

Willie McGinest Caps a Nail-Biter, Tripping Up Edgerrin James at the Goal Line

The game was as good as lost. The game probably *should have* been lost.

The Patriots had undone themselves. They hadn't merely squandered the 31–10 lead they'd taken midway through the third quarter, they had allowed the Indianapolis Colts to set up on the New England goal line with 52 seconds on the clock. Indy, now trailing 38–34, would have four chances to advance the ball into the end zone. And when the Colts scored, they would leave way too little time on the clock for the visiting Patriots offense to do anything.

You could blame Ken Walter if you wanted. Walter had presented Peyton Manning and the Colts offense with a great opportunity to complete their comeback victory when he shanked a punt from the New England 30 with 2:57 left in the game. The Colts took over at the Patriots' 48. It

took them six plays and two minutes of game time to get to the goal line.

On a team with the guiding philosophy that wins come from players doing their jobs, an 18-yard punt in crunch time was unforgivable.

Still, three minutes would have been plenty of time for the Colts offense no matter how well Walter had punted. And it certainly wasn't Walter who had let Indianapolis back into the game to begin with. The fault for that rested as much with Tom Brady as it did anyone.

Brady threw a pair of third-quarter picks, each of which Manning converted to seven points. The first of them—deflected off the hand of wide receiver Bethel Johnson and intercepted by safety Donald Strickland at the Colts' 17-yard line—took at least three Patriots points off the board. The second, cut off and snatched by cornerback

**Edgerrin James picks up a first down for the Colts at the Patriots' goal line with 52 seconds remaining. James and the Colts would get no further.** *Photo courtesy of Getty Images.*

Nick Harper at the New England 26, set up an easy Indianapolis touchdown.

Points resulting from Brady's miscues accounted for all of the Colts' scoring in the third quarter and most of the work Indy needed to do to get back in the game.

Yet another turnover, a fumble by running back Kevin Faulk recovered by defensive end Raheem Brock at the Patriots' 12, set up a field goal that cut the Pats' lead to 38–34.

It felt like the offense was doing everything it could to give the game away.

The defense faltered in the second half, too. But that will happen when you face the Colts, particularly when you repeatedly give Manning short fields to work with. The *D* spent a lot of time on the field late in the game. During the final Colts drive, the signs of wear were unmistakable.

All the less reason, then, to hope the *D* could possibly hold with the Colts a yard away from a game-winning touchdown.

But then they held on first down. Manning handed off to Edgerrin James, who tried to run behind the right guard and was stuffed by a committee of linebackers and defensive backs led by Tedy Bruschi and Rodney Harrison.

They held on second, too, swarming James as he tried to squeeze through the two gap.

On third, Manning looked for receiver Aaron Moorehead on a fade left, but Tyrone Poole had Moorehead in tight coverage, and the pass sailed overhead and out of bounds.

Then came fourth-and-goal. And every heart in the RCA Dome and in every bar and living room in New England came to a temporary stop. The team that prevailed would go to 10–2 and take the inside track for the AFC one-seed. The team that failed would drop to 9–3.

The Colts lined up in a pass formation. Willie McGinest positioned himself as if to cover the slot receiver. Then McGinest saw evidence of what he knew was coming: Manning signaled a checkdown to the run.

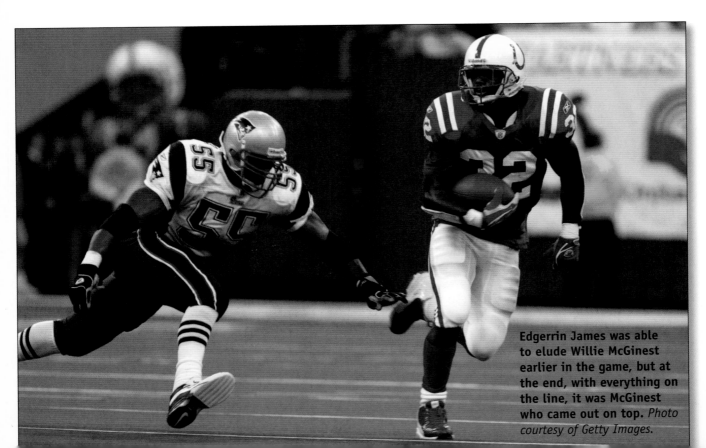

**Edgerrin James was able to elude Willie McGinest earlier in the game, but at the end, with everything on the line, it was McGinest who came out on top.** *Photo courtesy of Getty Images.*

Just before the snap, McGinest slid two steps closer to the center. And as Manning took the ball, McGinest bolted unblocked around the right side of the Colts line. He snagged James by the legs just after the handoff, wrapping his arms around the running back's knees and dragging him to the turf. The Colts' last try for six had failed. The game was over.

A Patriots defense that hadn't mounted a successful goal-line stand all season had somehow managed to shut down the league's second-ranked offense on four consecutive goal-to-go plays. It was a phenomenal moment for the Patriots.

The win wasn't pretty. But it was exciting. It was decisive. It was pivotal.

It was a win, and that was enough.

# Game Details

## New England Patriots 38 • Indianapolis Colts 34

| Patriots | 10 | 14 | 7 | 7 | 38 |
|----------|----|----|---|---|----|
| Colts | 0 | 10 | 14 | 10 | 34 |

**Date:** November 30, 2003

**Team Records:** Patriots 10–2; Colts 9–3

**Scoring Plays:**

NE Vinatieri 43-yard FG

NE Cloud 4-yard run (Vinatieri PAT)

NE Ward 31-yard pass from Brady (Vinatieri PAT)

IND Vanderjagt 40-yard FG

IND Pollard 8-yard pass from Manning (Vanderjagt PAT)

NE Johnson 92-yard kickoff return (Vinatieri PAT)

NE Cloud 1-yard run (Vinatieri PAT)

IND Wayne 13-yard pass from Manning (Vanderjagt PAT)

IND Harrison 26-yard pass from Manning (Vanderjagt PAT)

IND Walters 6-yard pass from Manning (Vanderjagt PAT)

NE Branch 13-yard pass from Brady (Vinatieri PAT)

IND Vanderjagt 29-yard FG

# There's Always Next Time

Even as the teams walked off the field at the RCA Dome November 30, you knew it wasn't over between the Patriots and Colts. The teams were destined to meet again in January with a lot more than the best record in the conference on the line.

The AFC Championship Game was played at snowy Gillette Stadium on January 18, 2004. And it couldn't have been a more different game than the regular-season tilt.

The Patriots took control on the opening drive, marching from their 35 to the Colts' end zone and eating up seven minutes of game time. At the end of their first series of downs, the Pats faced fourth-and-one at their own 44. Tom Brady picked up the first down with a quarterback sneak. The play put the Colts on notice that the Pats planned to outphysical them, which was precisely what happened.

Peyton Manning threw four interceptions, three of them to cornerback Ty Law. But it was really Manning's first pick, grabbed by Rodney Harrison in the end zone, that broke Indy's back. Manning, who had completed 79 percent of his passes in postseason wins over Denver and Kansas City, wasn't going to have such an easy time against New England.

The Pats led 15–0 at halftime. And while the Colts managed to score twice in the second half, the outcome was never truly in question. The Pats took the conference title with a 24–14 win and headed for Houston to face the Carolina Panthers in Super Bowl XXXVIII.

**Great players make great plays at key moments.**
**—GIL SANTOS**

September 9, 2004

# The Sack

McGinest Steps Up with a Sack That Sets the Tone for a Season

You wouldn't want to say the Colts were *owned* by the Patriots.

Well, you might want to say that, but you wouldn't actually do it if you were smart. It wasn't like the Pats kept running away with wins over Indy. They just kept finding ways to come out ahead in the end.

Starting with Tom Brady's first game as a starter, the Patriots beat the Colts six times straight, a run that included two key postseason victories. Only once, however, did the Pats honestly blow the Colts out.

More often, Indy at least found ways to keep things interesting. And twice, it took a major defensive effort in the closing minute to preserve a Patriots win.

On both of those occasions, Willie McGinest made the play that saved the game.

In 2003, when the New England *D* was forced to mount a goal-line stand in the final seconds of an action-packed road game, it was McGinest who made the final stop, wrapping up Colts running back Edgerrin James behind the line of scrimmage on fourth down.

And in the 2004 season opener, with the Colts in Foxborough looking to avenge a demoralizing loss to the Pats in the 2003–04 AFC Championship Game, it was again McGinest who stepped up.

Not that McGinest was any stranger to big plays. A standout defensive end at USC, McGinest was taken by the Patriots as the fourth overall pick in the 1994 draft. The Pats converted him to outside linebacker to take advantage of his speed and ferocity as an edge rusher. And he didn't disappoint.

In his second season with the Patriots, his first as a full-time starter, McGinest led the team with 11 sacks. In 1996 he was a key contributor to the AFC championship squad, recording another 9.5 sacks. Moving back and forth between linebacker and end, he made 78 sacks, forced 16 fumbles, and picked off four balls over his 12 years in a Patriots uniform. McGinest retired as the NFL record holder in postseason sacks, with 16. His 4.5 sacks against the Jacksonville Jaguars in the 2006–07 playoffs also set a league record.

It's hard to view a play in the first game of any season as particularly big, but McGinest managed one of those against the Colts.

The Colts, who closed the gap to 27–24 early in the fourth quarter before a string of turnovers by both teams

Willie McGinest shows Peyton Manning who's boss with a punishing sack that costs the Colts a chance to force overtime. *Photo courtesy of AP Images.*

shut down all scoring, were deep in Patriots territory, looking for the go-ahead touchdown or at least a field goal to force overtime.

With 49 seconds to play, the Colts faced third-and-eight at the New England 17. As Peyton Manning lined up in the shotgun, it appeared the worst-case scenario for his team was an incompletion followed by an easy shot for Mike Vanderjagt, who had been good on 42 straight field goals.

But then McGinest shot into the backfield and hammered Manning at the 29.

The 12-yard loss pushed Vanderjagt's attempt to 48 yards. And the kicker missed just right.

Once again, a big play by McGinest had spelled doom for Indianapolis. The Patriots may not have owned the Colts, but Willie McGinest sure did.

Willie McGinest (top), Tedy Bruschi (with ball), and Ty Law celebrate a great win to open the 2004 campaign. *Photo courtesy of Getty Images.*

> **W**illie McGinest's sack was one of the most memorable sacks in the history of the Patriots. Loved the squirming, disgusted body language that Peyton Manning displayed before and after play.
>
> —BOB HYLDBURG, AUTHOR OF *TOTAL PATRIOTS*

# Game Details

**New England Patriots 27 • Indianapolis Colts 24**

| | | | | | |
|---|---|---|---|---|---|
| Patriots | 3 | 10 | 14 | 0 | **27** |
| Colts | 0 | 17 | 0 | 7 | **24** |

**Date:** September 9, 2004

**Team Records:** Patriots 1–0; Colts 0–1

**Scoring Plays:**

NE Vinatieri 32-yard FG

IND Vanderjagt 32-yard FG

IND Rhodes 3-yard run (Vanderjagt PAT)

NE Branch 16-yard pass from Brady (Vinatieri PAT)

IND Harrison 3-yard pass from Manning (Vanderjagt PAT)

NE Vinatieri 43-yard FG

NE Patten 25-yard pass from Brady (Vinatieri PAT)

NE Graham 8-yard pass from Brady (Vinatieri PAT)

IND Stokley 7-yard pass from Manning (Vanderjagt PAT)

# Brady's Pats vs. Manning's Colts: The Story In Brief

**September 30, 2001**
Foxboro Stadium
Patriots 44, Colts 13
*Defining play:* Otis Smith returned an interception 78 yards for a touchdown.

**November 30, 2003**
RCA Dome
Patriots 38, Colts 34
*Defining play:* Willie McGinest stopped Edgerrin James on fourth-and-goal with 11 seconds remaining.

**January 18, 2004**
Gillette Stadium
Patriots 24, Colts 14
AFC Championship Game
*Defining play:* Tom Brady converted a fourth-and-one at the Patriots' 44-yard line on the opening drive.

**September 9, 2004**
Gillette Stadium
Patriots 27, Colts 24
*Defining play:* Willie McGinest sacked Peyton Manning at the Patriots' 29 for a 12-yard loss on third down.

**January 16, 2005**
Gillette Stadium
Patriots 20, Colts 3
Divisional Round Playoff
*Defining play:* Tedy Bruschi forced and recovered a Dominic Rhodes fumble.

**November 7, 2005**
Gillette Stadium
Colts 40, Patriots 21
*Defining play:* Backup quarterback Doug Flutie lost a fumble on third down as time expired.

**November 5, 2006**
Gillette Stadium
Colts 27, Patriots 20
*Defining play:* Cato June intercepted a Tom Brady pass at the Colts 32-yard line with 1:18 remaining.

**January 21, 2007**
RCA Dome
Colts 38, Patriots 34
AFC Championship Game
*Defining play:* Wide-open Reche Caldwell dropped a pass with a clear path to the end zone.

**November 4, 2007**
RCA Dome
Patriots 24, Colts 20
*Defining play:* Kevin Faulk beat three defenders on a run-after-catch touchdown late in the fourth quarter.

**November 2, 2008**
Lucas Oil Stadium
Colts 18, Patriots 15
*Defining play:* Adam Vinatieri put the winning points on the board with a 52-yard field goal.

**November 15, 2009**
Lucas Oil Stadium
Colts 35, Patriots 34
*Defining play:* The Patriots failed to convert on fourth-and-two at their own 28 with two minutes remaining.

January 16, 2005

# Give Me That

Bruschi's Rip Sets the Tone for a Punishing Win Over Indianapolis

Tedy Bruschi said, "No."

He looked at Dominic Rhodes and Peyton Manning and the whole Indianapolis Colts offense, and he told them it wasn't their day. No matter what they might have come into Foxborough thinking, the Colts weren't going to be the team to stop the Patriots from repeating as Super Bowl champions.

It didn't matter that the New England offense wasn't finishing drives. It didn't matter that the Patriots defense was up against the league's highest-scoring offense and without the services of its best pass rusher, Richard Seymour, and both of its starting cornerbacks, Ty Law and Tyrone Poole. And it sure as hell didn't matter that Colts kicker Mike Vanderjagt thought the Patriots were "ripe for the picking."

The Pats had muscled their way to a 14–2 record even as their defense lost one player after another to injury. They were the conference two-seed. They were at home and coming off a bye. They weren't losing. No matter what. Bruschi and his defensive unit, cobbled together though it might have been, simply weren't going to allow it.

And just in case 27 minutes of scoreless football hadn't quite gotten the point across to an offense that averaged 33 points a game in the regular season, Bruschi took it on himself to clarify things as the end of the first half approached.

The Colts had managed to fight their way into New England territory for the first time in the game. Trailing 6–0 by virtue of a pair of Adam Vinatieri field goals, Indianapolis was pushing steadily through the wet snow that had been falling throughout the late afternoon. On the strength of Edgerrin James' running and Manning's short

Tedy Bruschi shows off the ball he refused to let Dominic Rhodes hold on to. *Photo courtesy of Getty Images.*

passes to Brandon Stokley, Reggie Wayne, and Marvin Harrison, the Colts had reached the Patriots' 29-yard line.

After a holding call, the Colts faced second-and-17 from the 39.

Manning dropped back and tossed a quick pass to the tailback Rhodes, who started to turn upfield but was hit immediately by Bruschi. But the linebacker didn't simply drive Rhodes to the ground, he hung the runner up and grabbed the ball. The players struggled as they fell— Bruschi yanking the ball, Rhodes trying desperately to hold on—but when they hit the ground, there was Bruschi on his back, ball clutched to his chest.

The message had been sent. Manning may have broken Dan Marino's record for most touchdown passes in a single season and taken league MVP honors for the second year running. The Colts may have led the league in scoring in the regular season. And they may have crushed the Denver Broncos 49–24 in the wild-card round. But this was New England, and the defending champions most assuredly were not ripe for the picking.

The Colts did find their way onto the scoreboard before the half was out. A drive that ran out of time before it ran out of downs ended with a 23-yard field goal by Vanderjagt in the final two seconds of the period.

But that was all the Colts would get.

In the second half, you would hardly have guessed the Patriots' *D* was missing so much as a situational backup. The secondary, in particular, played inspired football, hammering Colts receivers to the point where every catch was followed not by a survey upfield, but a wary glance over the shoulder. The Colts were allowed to accomplish nothing other than two more turnovers, both brought on by the always punishing play of Rodney Harrison.

> **E**very defense needs a guy who does more than just play his position, but is a leader on the field. Bruschi was a great leader on the field.
>
> —STEVE NELSON

Midway through the fourth quarter, Harrison blasted Wayne at the Colts' 32-yard line, knocking the ball loose. Bruschi was there to fall on it. And at the very end of the game, Harrison was there to deny the Colts even a meaningless touchdown, intercepting Manning in the Patriots' end zone with four seconds to play and the Pats up by 17.

The offense helped with long, run-centered drives that kept Manning and his unit off the field. Their two touchdown drives, of 87 and 94 yards, ate up a combined 15 minutes of game clock. In all, New England held the ball for 37 minutes. And that, along with the defensive clampdown, did the trick.

The Colts, a team that hadn't scored fewer than 20 points in a meaningful game all season, left with three on the board and their tails between their legs.

"That game established the early story line that Bill Belichick was in Peyton Manning's head, that Peyton couldn't beat the Patriots," says Bob Kravitz, sports columnist for *The Indianapolis Star*, noting, of course, that the Colts would turn things around just two years later.

But two years later wasn't on the minds of the Patriots that night. All the Pats were thinking about was the fact that the 16–1 Steelers were waiting for them.

# Game Details

### New England Patriots 20 • Indianapolis Colts 3

| Patriots | 0 | 6 | 7 | 7 | **20** |
|---|---|---|---|---|---|
| Colts | 0 | 3 | 0 | 0 | **3** |

**Date:** January 16, 2005
**Team Records:** Patriots 15–2; Colts 13–5
**Scoring Plays:**
NE Vinatieri 24-yard FG
NE Vinatieri 31-yard FG
IND Vanerjagt 23-yard FG
NE Givens 5-yard pass from Brady (Vinatieri PAT)
NE Brady 1-yard run (Vinatieri PAT)

# Clock-Killin' Corey Dillon

Eight seasons into a stellar NFL career, Corey Dillon had a new nickname. Clock-Killin' Dillon, his teammates called him. In their playoff matchup with the Colts, Dillon carried the ball 23 times for 144 yards, eating up all kinds of game time. Most of Dillon's yardage came four, five, and six yards at a pop, though he did have a spectacular 42-yard carry on a sweep in the second quarter and, in the fourth, a carry up the middle and past what seemed like every Colts defender on the field 27 yards to the Indianapolis 1-yard line.

Dillon got something more important than a nickname against the Colts, though. He got vindication in the form of his first-ever postseason appearance. Dillon spent his first seven NFL seasons with the Cincinnati Bengals. He played well, racking up rushing totals of better than 1,300 and 1,400 yards and making three Pro Bowl appearances. But he was the whole of the Bengals' offense, and the results were predictable. The team was 34–78 overall during Dillon's time in Cincinnati.

Dillon was viewed as a malcontent by the time he jawed his way out of that losing situation, but he fit perfectly into New England's team-first atmosphere. And he played his best football with the Pats. In 2004, his first season in New England, Dillon amassed a franchise-record 1,635 rushing yards. And against the Colts he more than proved the value of the second-round pick the Pats had traded to get him.

**With the Patriots, Corey Dillon no longer had to be his team's whole offense, which freed him to play his best football.** *Photo courtesy of AP Images.*

**Rodney Harrison's fourth-quarter interception of Jaguars quarterback David Garrard sealed a playoff win for the Patriots.** *Photo courtesy of Getty Images.*

January 12, 2008

# And Defense, Too

Rodney Harrison Ties a Record and Seals a Playoff Win with a Big Pick

It was all about offense for the 2007 New England Patriots. All about gaudy stats and new league records. All about Brady-to-Moss and Brady-to-Welker and see if you can stop us from doing it again.

It was fun to watch. But so had been the teams of 2001, '03, and '04. The squads built on defense, Bill Belichick's stock in trade. The teams that would have torn an opposing player's hands off if it was going to give them a shot at the ball.

It was nice every now and then to see plays that reminded you of those seasons. Once or twice during the push to Super Bowl XLII, those plays actually proved important.

And once again, when big defensive plays were in order, the Pats looked to Rodney Harrison.

It was good to have that luxury. Harrison had missed the playoffs in each of the previous two seasons. Knee injuries had sidelined him through most of the 2005 campaign and again just in time for the 2006–07 playoffs. His absence alone hadn't accounted for the team's divisional-round loss to the Denver Broncos or its collapse against the

Indianapolis Colts in the AFC Championship Game, but you certainly couldn't argue that the Patriots were a better team without Harrison.

As the Patriots, coming off a first-round bye, hosted the Jacksonville Jaguars in the divisional round of the 2006–07 playoffs, Harrison made his first postseason start since his huge two-interception outing in Super Bowl XXXIX.

He picked up exactly where he left off, delivering hard hits throughout the game and making spectacular plays on the ball in clutch situations. He committed a pair of costly penalties, but he made up for both with big plays later in the same drives.

Early in the fourth quarter, with the Jaguars trailing 28–17, Harrison hit Ernest Wilford when the wide receiver was already down, tacking 15 yards on to the end of a first-down play and advancing the Jags to their 42-yard line. But when Jacksonville quarterback David Garrard tried to find Reggie Williams at the back of the end zone on second-and-goal from the 7, Harrison was there to stop the score. With his back to the quarterback, Harrison stuck a

Rodney Harrison (right) and Randy Moss celebrate the interception that ensured the Patriots' record would improve to **17–0.** *Photo courtesy of Getty Images.*

# Visiting the Statue of Liberty

It's not like New England's high-powered offense shut down in the first game of the 2007–08 playoffs. Rodney Harrison and the defense had to work harder than they had through most of the regular season to preserve a win, but there were plenty of big plays on the other side of the ball as well.

The most memorable moment for the offense came early in the third quarter. With the score tied and the Patriots threatening on first-and-goal at the Jacksonville 6-yard line, the team rolled out a variation on the rarely seen Statue of Liberty play. Tom Brady took the snap out of the shotgun, faked a handoff to running back Kevin Faulk, and spun with his back to the defense, hand raised in the air as if

he were faking a high snap to decoy for the run. The defensive front bit and swarmed Faulk at the line of scrimmage. Meanwhile, slot receiver Wes Welker, after feigning a run block, cut out around his supposed linebacker assignment and headed for the back of the end zone. Brady turned back around and fired to Welker, who pulled in the touchdown, putting the Patriots ahead 21–14.

The Jaguars were able to close the gap to four with a Josh Scobee field goal on their next possession. But a nine-yard touchdown pass from Brady to Benjamin Watson at the end of the quarter put the Pats on top by 11. The defense took it from there.

hand in the air and batted the ball away before it could reach its target.

The play helped limit Jacksonville to a field goal, a score New England kicker Stephen Gostkowski matched at the end of the Pats' drive that followed.

The Jaguars were trying desperately to get back in the game when another Harrison roughing penalty—this time for a late hit out of bounds on wide receiver Dennis Northcutt—again gave them a free 15 yards.

Four plays later, however, as Garrard tried desperately to convert a fourth-and-six from the Patriots' 41, Harrison cut off a pass aimed at Matt Jones and made a pick that sealed the victory.

The interception was Harrison's seventh in the post-season, a team record. It also marked Harrison's fourth consecutive playoff game with at least one pick, tying a league record held by Aeneas Williams.

Most important, it ensured the Pats of their 17th victory, moving them to within two wins of perfection. And with Rodney Harrison back on board in the secondary, you could believe they had a real shot.

## Game Details

**New England Patriots 31 • Jacksonville Jaguars 20**

| | | | | | |
|---|---|---|---|---|---|
| **Patriots** | 7 | 7 | 14 | 3 | **31** |
| **Jaguars** | 7 | 7 | 3 | 3 | **20** |

**Date:** January 12, 2008

**Team Records:** Patriots 17–0; Jaguars 12–6

**Scoring Plays:**

JAC Jones 8-yard pass from Garrard (Scobee PAT)

NE Watson 3-yard pass from Brady (Gostkowski PAT)

NE Maroney 1-yard run (Gostkowski PAT)

JAC Wilford 6-yard pass from Garrard (Scobee PAT)

NE Welker 6-yard pass from Brady (Gostkowski PAT)

JAC Scobee 39-yard FG

NE Watson 9-yard pass from Brady (Gostkowski PAT)

JAC Scobee 25-yard FG

NE Gostkowski 35-yard FG

# Special Consideration

December 28, 1985

# Wild Wild Card

Fumble-Return Touchdown Spurs a
Postseason Turnover Frenzy

If you had said ahead of time that the 1985
Patriots' wild-card weekend trip to the
Meadowlands was just the beginning of a push
to Super Bowl XX, you'd have been labeled a
hopeless homer. And with good reason. No
team had ever managed to reach the Super
Bowl by way of three postseason road wins,
and there was no real reason to suspect the
Patriots could be the first.

As it turns out, New Orleans and the Super Bowl
were exactly where the Pats were headed. And it was
plays like the one Johnny Rembert made late in the third
quarter against the New York Jets that made the difference in all three of New England's playoff victories. It was
turnovers that landed a franchise that hadn't won a postseason game in 22 years on the NFL's biggest stage. And
even though the eventual outcome, a crushing defeat at
the hands of the Chicago Bears, was unsatisfying to say
the least, the fight to get there is something fans who saw
it will never forget.

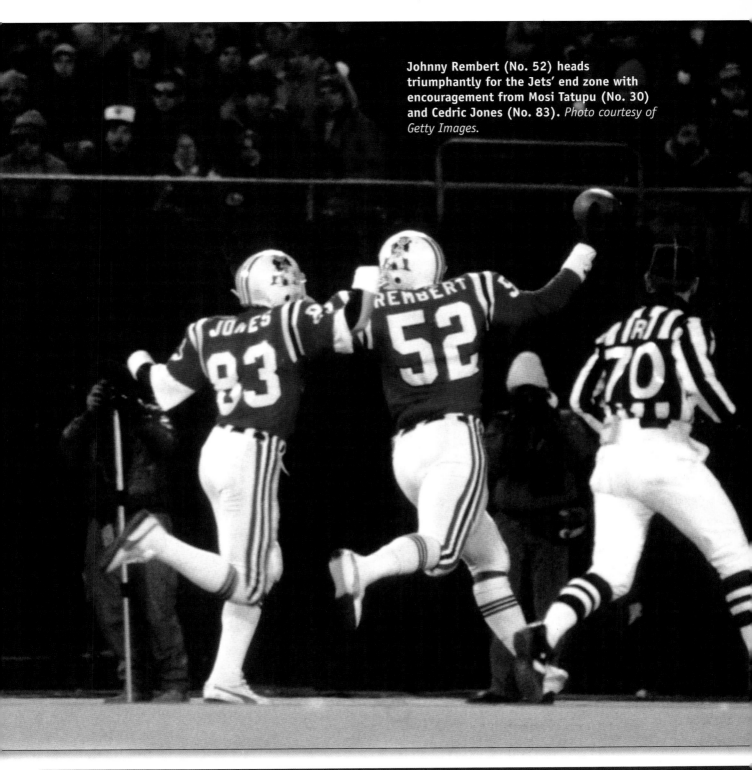

Johnny Rembert (No. 52) heads triumphantly for the Jets' end zone with encouragement from Mosi Tatupu (No. 30) and Cedric Jones (No. 83). *Photo courtesy of Getty Images.*

> **I**n three playoff games, we ended up getting at least eight fumble recoveries and scored twice. It was one of the most significant edges we had.
>
> —RAYMOND BERRY

Tony Franklin's barefoot style was quirky, but Franklin was one of the many special teamers who made a major contribution to the 1985 Patriots' run to the Super Bowl. *Photo courtesy of AP Images.*

The Pats went into New Jersey as three-point underdogs. They had secured the AFC's final wild-card spot only a week earlier.

The Jets were a wild-card team, too, having finished the season with the same record as the Pats, 11-5. But they'd beaten the Patriots 16-13 in the teams' regular-season meeting at Giants Stadium. And the Jets were home again.

But it wasn't *where* the game was played but *how* that mattered to the Patriots. They made sure it was played their way: with hard hits, hustle, and sound fundamentals. Their focus, as it had been since Raymond Berry took over as head coach midway through the previous season, was on keeping the ball when it was theirs and taking it away when it was their opponent's.

That focus would pay off again and again in the AFC playoffs, starting with a heads-up special-teams effort by Rembert.

The play came on a kickoff that followed a 20-yard Tony Franklin field goal that had put the Pats ahead 16-7 with a little more than five minutes to play in the third.

Jets running back Johnny Hector fielded the kick at the 3-yard line and advanced the ball to the 16 before he was hit by Rembert, who reached in and popped the ball out of Hector's hands.

As Hector fell backward, the ball bounced up off his helmet and tumbled back down into Rembert's hands. Rembert snagged the ball and rolled away from Hector. Prompted by his teammates, he popped back onto his feet and bolted for the end zone.

"I didn't go out there to score," Rembert recalls. "All I wanted to do was make the tackle. On special teams, there were a few of us—me, Mosi Tatupu, Ed Reynolds, and Jim Bowman—who were always trying to compete to see who could get down there quickest and make the tackle. So that's what I was trying to do. But then when I was making the tackle I just kind of pulled the ball. I saw it coming out and then it just bounced right to me."

Rembert's 15-yard return TD put the Pats ahead 23-7, effectively sealing a victory. It remains one of the most exciting moments in an astounding run that would see the Pats take the ball away 16 times in three AFC playoff games.

The turnover fest wouldn't last long enough to make much of a difference in the Super Bowl, but it would make the push to New Orleans a lot of fun. And that's something.

# Game Details

**New England Patriots 26 • New York Jets 14**

| Patriots | 3 | 10 | 10 | 3 | **26** |
|---|---|---|---|---|---|
| Jets | 0 | 7 | 7 | 0 | **14** |

**Date:** December 28, 1985

**Team Records:** Patriots 12–5; Jets 11–6

**Scoring Plays:**

NE Franklin 33-yard FG

NYJ Hector 11-yard pass from O'Brien (Leahy PAT)

NE Franklin 41-yard FG

NE Morgan 36-yard pass from Eason (Franklin PAT)

NE Franklin 20-yard FG

NE Rembert 15-yard fumble return (Franklin PAT)

NYJ Shuler 12-yard pass from Ryan (Leahy PAT)

NE Franklin 26-yard FG

# Squishing the Fish

There's no overstating the importance of the 1985 Patriots' playoff victories over the Jets in New Jersey and the Raiders in Los Angeles. The former was the first postseason win by the Patriots since 1963. The latter went a good way toward avenging the apparent win that had been stolen from the 1976 squad. But there's also no denying that the biggest victory recorded by the 1985 Patriots was their AFC championship defeat of the Miami Dolphins. And no, that's not just because beating the Dolphins propelled the Pats to their first Super Bowl berth. The Patriots showed up in Miami on January 12, 1986, having lost to the Dolphins in South Florida 18 consecutive times, including in a regular-season game played less than a month earlier. The Pats were playing on the road for the third straight week. They went into Miami as six-point underdogs. But when the teams took the field, nothing happened the way it was supposed to. The Patriots scored first, went into halftime with a 17–7 lead, held onto the ball for better than 40 minutes, and took the ball away six times, recovering four fumbles and picking off Dolphins quarterback Dan Marino twice. The Pats captured the AFC championship by a score of 31–17, beginning a period in which they would make six trips to the Super Bowl in 23 years (the most appearances by any team during that stretch). And they made fans in *Squish the Fish* T-shirts all over New England very happy.

> **O**nce I had it, I didn't know if I was down. But then I heard Mosi calling. He was pulling on me, yelling "Get up! Get up!" So I got up.
>
> —JOHNNY REMBERT

**Cedric Jones (left) and Jim Bowman (middle) scramble for the ball as the Raiders' Sam Seale makes a last-ditch attempt to make up for his kickoff-return fumble.** *Photo courtesy of Getty Images.*

# Turnaround by Turnover

## Fumble Recovery Touchdown Leads to Victory and Sweet Revenge

In the minds of many, the postseason story of the Patriots and the Raiders is written in two chapters. In the first, the Raiders, with help from referee Ben Dreith, steal a victory—and probably a Super Bowl championship—from the 1976 Patriots. And in the last (at least for now), the Patriots—powered by the amazing leg of Adam Vinatieri—turn things around, coming from behind to beat the Raiders in overtime and beginning a march down the road to dynasty.

It's an understandable way of looking at things, but it's wrong. There's a middle chapter, and a sweet one at that. It's a chapter in which the fundamentally sound and chronically underrated 1985 Patriots travel to Los Angeles, then home of the Raiders, and earn a come-from-behind divisional playoff victory over a team that was supposed to be Super Bowl bound. And it turns on a heads-up play that, for a while at least, made a regional folk hero of a rookie special-teamer who did what he was supposed to do—at the precise moment his team needed it most.

What Jim Bowman did was something he'd been trained to do all season. He chased down and recovered a fumble. The recovery, which came on a kickoff following a game-tying field goal by Tony Franklin, took place in the Raiders' end zone. With Franklin's successful extra point, it put the Patriots ahead 27–20 late in the third quarter. And 27–20 was the score by which the Patriots would win that game, propelling them on to an AFC Championship Game against the Miami Dolphins and, ultimately, to their first Super Bowl berth.

Bowman, like the rest of the 1985 Patriots, had been trained extensively in the art of forcing and recovering fumbles. It was a point of emphasis for head coach Raymond Berry, then in his first full season running the Patriots. Berry took it as a point of pride that he'd fumbled only once in his 13-year Hall of Fame career as a wide receiver. He stressed repeatedly to his team that turnovers could decide games. The point was driven home by the fact that the Pats recorded key regular-season wins and playoff victories alike on the backs of forced turnovers.

Against the heavily favored Raiders, the AFC's top-seeded team, the wild-card Patriots intercepted three Marc Wilson passes and recovered three fumbles. Bowman was responsible for two of those recoveries.

The first came on a punt dropped by Fulton Walker in the first quarter. Bowman's recovery at the Raiders' 21-yard line set up a touchdown pass from Tony Eason to Lin Dawson that put the Patriots ahead 7–0.

The second, the game decider, came on the heels of a comeback from the 17–7 deficit the Patriots found them-selves in midway through the second quarter. After battling back to trail 20–17 at halftime, the Patriots posted the first points of the third quarter in Franklin's 32-yard field goal, tying the score with 1:11 remaining in the period.

Raiders return man Sam Seale took the ensuing kickoff at his 9, dropped the ball, and picked it up again just in time to get slammed by Mosi Tatupu. The hit jarred the ball loose, and as it bounced toward the end zone, Bowman and his teammate Cedric Jones gave chase.

"Cedric ended up tapping it into the end zone, and I just sort of fell on it," Bowman says, laughing. "That's my big play."

One small dose of sound fundamentals for a football player. One giant hunk of revenge for his franchise.

> **H**ow to handle a fumbled ball was something we worked on all season. Jim was in the right place when it happened, but he knew what to do.
>
> **—RAYMOND BERRY**

# Game Details

## New England Patriots 27 • Los Angeles Raiders 20

| Patriots | 7 | 10 | 10 | 0 | **27** |
|---|---|---|---|---|---|
| Raiders | 3 | 17 | 0 | 0 | **20** |

**Date:** January 5, 1986

**Team Records:** Patriots 13–5; Raiders 12–5

**Scoring Plays:**

NE Dawson 13-yard pass from Eason (Franklin PAT)

LA Bahr 29-yard FG

LA Hester 16-yard pass from Wilson (Bahr PAT)

LA Allen 11-yard run (Bahr PAT)

NE James 2-yard run (Franklin PAT)

NE Franklin 45-yard FG

LA Bahr 32-yard FG

NE Franklin 32-yard FG

NE Bowman fumble recovery in end zone (Franklin PAT)

# Jim Bowman

Aside from his big moment in the spotlight during the 1985 Patriots' run to Super Bowl XX, Jim Bowman's career in professional football was solid but unspectacular. Bowman was a consistent contributor on special teams and had his moments in the defensive backfield, logging a pair of picks during a Patriots win against the Indianapolis Colts in 1987 and pulling down a game-clinching interception at the Patriots' 5-yard line against the Super Bowl–bound Cincinnati Bengals in 1988 (ensuring the Bengals their first loss after a 6–0 start). But he never stood out again like he did in Los Angeles. And a knee injury ended his career after five seasons. Two decades after he last suited up, however, it's possible to spot Bowman on the sideline in Foxborough on game days. Since 1997 Bowman has served as an NFL uniform inspector. His job is to make sure every player and every coach is dressed in accordance with league standards. He makes sure Tom Brady's socks are pulled up, Vince Wilfork's shirt is tucked in, and Bill Belichick's hoodie is...well, that it lives up to whatever scant standards it's supposed to live up to. Apparently, Bowman does a pretty good job. In February 2009, he was tapped to perform uniform inspection duties at the Pro Bowl in Honolulu, Hawaii, an honor he never received as a player. "It's the greatest part-time job ever created," says Bowman, who works in sales for a wine distributor during the week.

**Jim Bowman (No. 28) celebrates his go-ahead fumble-recovery touchdown with teammates, including Cedric Jones (No. 83) and Brian Ingram (No. 51).**
*Photo courtesy of Getty Images.*

> **M**y role that year was special teams, and you certainly take a lot of pride in your job. You're not looking for plays like that, but when they come and you make them, you feel good about it.
>
> —JIM BOWMAN

January 27, 2002

# Everybody Wants Some

Heads-Up Special-Teams Play Gives the Patriots an Insurmountable Lead

It went like this. The Patriots were ahead of the heavily favored Pittsburgh Steelers 14–3 early in the third quarter of the AFC Championship Game, but the game was anything but over.

Tom Brady was out, having gone down with a knee injury at the end of the first half. The Pats were lucky enough to have Drew Bledsoe as their backup quarterback, and he'd thrown a touchdown pass. But any quarterback could be expected to perform only so well against a Steelers defense that allowed just 184 passing yards and 13 points a game during the regular season.

And although Bledsoe undoubtedly knew how to win games, there was no way he wasn't rusty. He'd been on the sideline since late September when he was injured in a game against the New York Jets.

The hope was that the sixth-ranked New England defense would hold and that the offense would do enough to maintain their lead, but in postseason NFL football one can never assume a win is in the bag.

Plus, the Steelers were getting ready to close the gap to eight points. After a key stop by the defense prevented the Pats from converting on fourth down at the Steelers' 32-yard line, Pittsburgh had advanced the ball to the New England 16. The Steelers were lining up to try a 34-yard field goal, which should have been no problem for kicker Kris Brown.

Eight points. A touchdown and a two-point conversion, effectively one score.

Thing is, Brown's kick never got anywhere near the goal post. Patriots defensive lineman Brandon Mitchell

I knew it was a risk pitching it out, but I wanted to get the ball to Antwan. He was the fastest guy on the field.

—TROY BROWN

Brandon Mitchell (No. 96) blocks Steelers kicker Kris Brown's field-goal attempt.
*Photo courtesy of Getty Images.*

Troy Brown scoops up the loose ball as Kris Brown reaches out to try to make a tackle. *Photo courtesy of Getty Images.*

got a hand on the ball and sent it bouncing into the backfield. The Pats gave chase and Troy Brown scooped it up at the New England 40-yard line. He carried it just across midfield, where the kicker caught him by the shirttail and started to drag him down.

The block and recovery would have been enough. The kick-coverage team had taken three Steelers points off the board and set the offense up with great field position. Bledsoe's squad could have converted the play to three or seven for New England, and the Pats would have had a comfortable lead and the path to the Super Bowl would have begun to look clearer.

## Game Details

**New England Patriots 24 • Pittsburgh Steelers 17**

| | | | | | |
|---|---|---|---|---|---|
| Patriots | 7 | 7 | 7 | 3 | **24** |
| Steelers | 0 | 3 | 14 | 0 | **17** |

**Date:** January 27, 2002

**Team Records:** Patriots 13–5; Steelers 14–4

**Scoring Plays:**

NE Brown 55-yard punt return (Vinatieri PAT)

PIT Brown 30-yard FG

NE Patten 11-yard pass from Bledsoe (Vinatieri PAT)

NE Harris 49-yard blocked FG return (Vinatieri PAT)

PIT Bettis 1-yard run (Brown PAT)

PIT Zereoue 11-yard run (Brown PAT)

NE Vinatieri 44-yard FG

> **I**t feels good to look back on it. Not just that play, but the whole game. Our special teams won the game that day, and I was part of it.
>
> —ANTWAN HARRIS

Antwan Harris outraces Jerame Tuman of the Steelers en route to the end zone as Tedy Bruschi moves in to provide blocking help. *Photo courtesy of AP Images.*

But it didn't end there. Brown didn't just go down. He heard his teammate, defensive back Antwan Harris, calling for the ball. He looked left and lateraled to Harris, who took the pitch, cut back across the field, and raced 49 yards to the end zone. The Pats went ahead 21–3.

"I was always the scoop-and-score guy," Harris says. "On that play, we were all after the ball. Troy got there first, but then I could see that he was about to get tackled, so I just started yelling, 'Pitch it! Pitch it! Pitch it, Troy! Pitch it!'"

The touchdown put momentum solidly in the Patriots' favor. It didn't end the game—the Steelers rebounded and put up two touchdowns before the end of the third quarter—but the 18-point lead ultimately proved insurmountable.

With a 44-yard field goal by Adam Vinatieri early in the fourth quarter, the Patriots went up 24–17. The touchdown gap put pressure on the Steelers and specifically on quarterback Kordell Stewart, who threw picks to safeties Tebucky Jones and Lawyer Milloy on Pittsburgh's final two possessions.

The top-seeded Steelers were upended.

The Patriots lifted the Lamar Hunt trophy for the second time in six seasons and began preparing to meet the St. Louis Rams in Super Bowl XXXVI.

## And a Punt-Return TD

"Wait," Troy Brown says. "There was another play in that game that you're forgetting about." Probably not. No one who saw it is ever going to forget how Troy Brown put the first points of the 2001–02 AFC Championship Game on the board. Late in the first quarter, Brown took a punt at the Patriots' 45-yard line, cut through the middle of the Steelers coverage team, eluding tackle after tackle, and zipped to the end zone, swinging momentum to the visiting Patriots.

But Brown doesn't want to boast about his play. He wants to talk about the penalty that set it up. "Josh Miller had a great punt that rolled down the sideline away from me. It went out of bounds at about the 25. But there was a penalty and he had to punt again. And when they put the ball down, they put it on the wrong hash. He couldn't punt directionally the way he wanted. That's why I was able to field that second punt." Brown found out about that a few years later when Miller came to play for the Patriots and told him. He laughs about it now.

Brown doesn't point out that his catches accounted for 121 of the Pats' 217 total passing yards that day. Or that he had a 28-yard grab on third down that kept the team's only touchdown drive alive. What else *does* Brown say? Just this: "I felt pretty good about being able to help our team win that game." Yeah, Troy, that won't soon be forgotten either.

November 7, 2004

# That's Troy on the Edge

## Sneaky Vinatieri-to-Brown Touchdown Shows the Rams Who's Still Boss

Some plays stick with you because they're pivotal, some because they're spectacular, some because they're just plain fun. And there are probably few things in football that are as much fun to watch as a trick play.

Fun is what the Patriots—or at least Patriots fans—needed when the team rolled in to St. Louis on November 7, 2004. Fun and a victory.

The Pats were coming off a brutal defeat in Pittsburgh a week earlier. The 34–20 loss on Halloween wasn't exactly the end of the world. New England was 6–1 and had a tiebreaker edge over the New York Jets in the AFC East standings. But the game had given Pittsburgh, also 6–1, an early advantage in the race for the conference's top post-season seeding. And, weighing a bit more heavily at that moment, it had brought an end to the Patriots' historic 21-game winning streak.

There wasn't any real reason to panic, though mounting injury problems in the defensive secondary were certainly a cause for some concern. There was, however, plenty of need for something to elevate the spirits and shore up confidence.

A win over the struggling Rams—a team the Patriots had last faced in Super Bowl XXXVI—might not have been enough all by itself. A win over the Rams in which Pats place-kicker Adam Vinatieri personally accounted for as many points as the entire St. Louis offense was a sheep of an altogether different color. A win in which six of Vinatieri's 22 points came from a trick-play touchdown pass? That more than got the job done.

Vinatieri, who had ended the Rams' dreams of dynasty with a 48-yard field goal in the teams' previous meeting, proved a thorn in St. Louis's sides from early on in the game, hitting his first of four field goals from 43 yards out three and a half minutes into the first quarter. By halftime, he'd kicked three more field goals and an extra point.

Midway through the fourth quarter, the Rams offense had accomplished a lot of nothing and the Pats led 19–14. So there was little reason to expect anything more than a fifth three-point play when New England's kicking team took the field on fourth-and-goal from the St. Louis 4-yard line.

That's the main reason no one noticed Troy Brown lined up on the far left side of the field, almost on the sideline.

Adam Vinatieri kicked four field goals and threw a touchdown pass to help the Patriots bounce back from their first loss in 22 games with a victory over St. Louis. *Photo courtesy of AP Images.*

Troy Brown celebrates his trick-play touchdown reception. *Photo courtesy of Getty Images.*

"That was a play where you had to know the rules to make it work," Brown recalls. "I had to report eligible by coming inside the numbers and being seen by the referee, and then I could go back outside. I think when I did that, the Rams thought I was going off the field."

Long-snapper Lonie Paxton delivered the ball not to holder Josh Miller but directly to Vinatieri, who looked left and tossed the ball to Brown at the goal line. Rams cornerback Jerametrius Butler realized what was happening and tried to hustle down the line, but there was no getting there fast enough. Brown took a step backward into the end zone, and the Pats went ahead 26–14.

The Pats would add to their lead as the afternoon wore on. And their 40–22 win would launch a six-game winning streak that would give them the AFC East title.

## Game Details

### New England Patriots 40 • St. Louis Rams 22

| | | | | | |
|---|---|---|---|---|---|
| **Patriots** | 6 | 13 | 14 | 7 | **40** |
| **Rams** | 0 | 14 | 0 | 8 | **22** |

**Date:** November 7, 2004

**Team Records:** Patriots 7–1; Rams 4–4

**Scoring Plays:**

NE Vinatieri 43-yard FG

NE Vinatieri 31-yard FG

STL Little fumble recovery in end zone (Wilkins PAT)

NE Vrabel 2-yard pass from Brady (Vinatieri PAT)

STL Bruce 11-yard pass from Bulger (Wilkins PAT)

NE Vinatieri 45-yard FG

NE Vinatieri 36-yard FG

NE Brown 4-yard pass from Vinatieri (Vinatieri PAT)

NE Dillon 5-yard run (Vinatieri PAT)

STL Holt 16-yard pass from Bulger (Faulk run)

NE Johnson 4-yard pass from Brady (Vinatieri PAT)

More important, the win—and the fun the Pats had getting it—cast the loss to Pittsburgh in a new light. The time for endings was over. It was time to refocus on the big picture and prepare for an eventual return visit to the Steel City.

## Automatic Adam

The things that will keep Adam Vinatieri's name alive long after he finally walks away from football are his two Super Bowl–winning kicks and his spectacular game-tying effort against Oakland in the 2001–02 playoffs. It's unlikely Vinatieri would object to being remembered for those incredible plays alone. But there's a good bit more to Vinatieri's legacy—and, specifically, to his legacy as a Patriot—than just those moments.

Vinatieri is arguably the greatest clutch-kicker in the history of professional football. Vinatieri has put the go-ahead points on the board in the final minute of a game 20 times in his career. He's played in five Super Bowls (four with the Patriots, one with the Indianapolis Colts) and has four championship rings to show for it. Not surprisingly, he holds the records for most field goals (7) and most extra points (13) in the Super Bowl.

As Aaron Schatz of Football Outsiders points out, Vinatieri's numbers don't necessarily make him the best kicker ever. "Adam Vinatieri benefited from playing for Patriots teams that were not ultra-dominant," Schatz notes. "He had more clutch kicks than any other player because he had more opportunities for clutch kicks than any other player." But the fact remains that Vinatieri has always made kicks when it counted. And that means that when there's a discussion about history's greatest kickers, his name at least has to be part of it.

January 1, 2006

# Parting Gift

Doug Flutie Makes History with a Career-Ending Drop-Kick PAT

Gino Cappelletti is embarrassed it took him so long to figure out what was happening.

He shouldn't be. Cappelletti certainly wasn't the only one who wondered what in the world was going on as Doug Flutie trotted out onto the field with the kicking team late in the final game of the 2005 regular season. Cappelletti was certainly better informed than the majority of confused observers, but that hardly mattered. There was really no anticipating a play that hadn't been run in professional football for most of 60 years.

And, let's face it, no one—even the guys broadcasting the game—could possibly have been seriously tuned in to what was taking place on the field by that point.

It was midway through the fourth quarter of a thoroughly meaningless game against the Miami Dolphins in Foxborough. The Patriots had come into the game with the AFC East title won, the conference four-seed secured, and no hope of earning a better postseason slot. They were putting in an effort, but you wouldn't say they were going all out. Backup quarterback Matt Cassel had been running the offense since the start of the second quarter.

A nine-yard pass from Cassel to Tim Dwight had pulled New England to within six points of the Dolphins.

The situation called for nothing other than a run-of-the-mill extra point.

So it was more than a bit confusing to see Flutie, who was listed as the third-string quarterback but whose real role was to serve as a veteran advisor to Tom Brady.

Cappelletti was thrown just like everybody else.

"When you saw Doug Flutie going in, you thought, *Whoa, two-point conversion?*" Cappelletti recalls. "And then you saw him in the shotgun, and he's retreating. I mean, he went back like a punter would. And sure enough, just before the snap I thought, *He's going to drop-kick it. I thought* it but not in time to say it."

That's really not something Cappelletti should let gnaw at him too much. Virtually no one else realized what had happened. Even after the fact. Not until Cappelletti filled us in.

What happened on the field was that Flutie took the snap from Lonie Paxton; dropped the ball, point down, on the turf; then kicked it the second it bounced, sending it sailing through the uprights. It was the first successful drop kick in an NFL game since 1941—when Ray McLean booted one for the Chicago Bears in the 1941 league championship—and the first in professional football since Joe

Doug Flutie makes the final splash of his long, successful football career, executing a seldom-seen drop-kick extra point. *Photo courtesy of Getty Images.*

Vetrano of the San Francisco 49ers, then part of the All-America Football Conference, converted one in 1948.

The drop kick, a carryover from football's roots in rugby and soccer, isn't used in the American game, mainly because the oblong ball has an unpredictable bounce.

"It's hard to be consistent at," says Cappelletti, who knows a bit about kicking footballs. "And on the point after, you've got to be 100 percent."

## And One for Vinny, Too

The broad grin on Bill Belichick's face said it all. The coach, whose expression typically ranges from dour all the way to scowling, beamed as Doug Flutie's drop-kick extra-point attempt connected. The play wasn't going to win the game (the Patriots weren't going to win the game), but it was going to make the history books. And that clearly meant something to the coach. That and the very act of allowing a player who'd more than paid his dues a chance to go out on a great note.

Those very things were likely on Belichick's mind again a season later when he gave another veteran backup quarterback a chance to make NFL history. The Patriots were out ahead of the Tennessee Titans 33–23 in the final game of the 2006 season when Belichick pulled Matt Cassel in favor of Vinny Testaverde. The veteran quarterback, who had played for Belichick in Cleveland, took over with the Pats at the Titans' 36-yard line with two minutes to play. He threw three passes, the last of them a six-yard touchdown pass to Troy Brown. And with that score, Testaverde extended his NFL record string of seasons with at least one touchdown pass to 20. (He'd make it 21 while playing for Carolina in 2007, his real final season.) The score wasn't necessary, and the Titans didn't like it. But Belichick didn't owe the Titans anything. If he had debts, they were to Testaverde and the game. Those, he paid.

Still, it was something Flutie was trained to do. Something he practiced. And something that football historian Bill Belichick wanted to let the quarterback try. Flutie was in his 21st and final season of professional ball. It was a going-away present.

"We were going to do it a few weeks before against the Jets, but we just didn't have the opportunity," Paxton recalls. "I know Doug really wanted to do it."

So Flutie booted his way into the history books. And the fans who stuck around into the latter part of a game nobody cared about came away with something they'll never forget.

## Game Details

**New England Patriots 26 • Miami Dolphins 28**

| | | | | | |
|---|---|---|---|---|---|
| **Patriots** | 7 | 3 | 3 | 13 | **26** |
| **Dolphins** | 7 | 6 | 5 | 10 | **28** |

**Date:** January 1, 2006
**Team Records:** Patriots 10–6; Dolphins 9–7
**Scoring Plays:**
MIA Williams 2-yard run (Mare PAT)
NE Branch 11-yard pass from Brady (Vinatieri PAT)
MIA Mare 36-yard FG
MIA Mare 38-yard FG
NE Vinatieri 49-yard FG
MIA Mare 41-yard FG
NE Vinatieri 33-yard FG
MIA Safety, Cassel fumbles out of the end zone
MIA Booker 15-yard pass from Frerotte (Mare PAT)
NE Dwight 9-yard pass from Cassel (Flutie PAT)
MIA Mare 42-yard FG
NE Watson 9-yard pass from Cassel (pass failed)

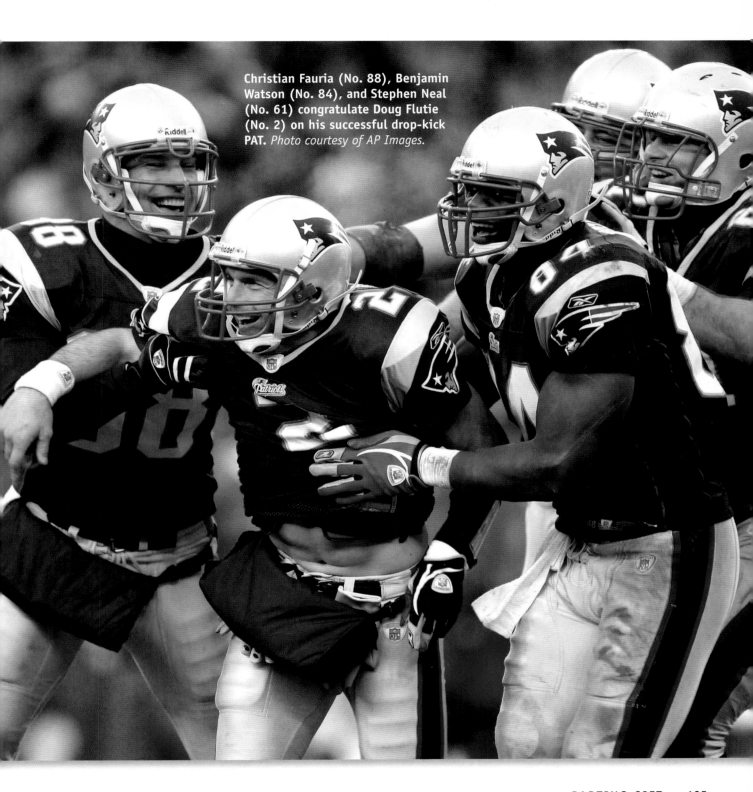

Christian Fauria (No. 88), Benjamin Watson (No. 84), and Stephen Neal (No. 61) congratulate Doug Flutie (No. 2) on his successful drop-kick PAT. *Photo courtesy of AP Images.*

September 9, 2007

# Take a Knee?

## Record-Setting Kick Return Sets the Tone for a Wild 2007 Season

The feeling lasted for maybe a couple of seconds. Maybe. But they were long seconds, the kind you only get during games. The kind that stretch out and give your sense of dread room to grow.

Ellis Hobbs had taken the opening kickoff of the second half eight yards deep in the Patriots' end zone. He'd seen the Jets coverage team flying toward him and then done the exact opposite of the sensible thing: He'd passed up a touchback and run the ball out of the end zone. You sensed it was a bad move as Hobbs emerged on the right side of the field. By the time he got to the 5, you *knew* it was a bad move.

The Jets' coverage team was closing in. Hobbs had effectively squandered a chance for the Patriots to extend their 14–7 lead. It was exactly what you didn't want to see happen against the Jets at the Meadowlands.

That was before anyone knew what to expect from the 2007 Patriots. New England wasn't a 16–0 team. They weren't even a 1–0 team. They were 0–0 and opening their season on the road against a division rival coached by a Bill Belichick protégé whose departure from New England had been rather less than pleasant.

What was known about the Pats was that they had collapsed in their last meaningful game, allowing the Indianapolis Colts to come back from an 18-point deficit to win the 2006–07 AFC Championship Game. They appeared to have improved in the off-season—adding wide receivers Randy Moss and Wes Welker—but there was no real knowing whether the moves would pan out.

Moss had been the best receiver in the league during his years in Minnesota, but he'd proven a disappointment after his trade to Oakland. So much so that the Raiders had

Ellis Hobbs breaks away on a path to a league-record 108-yard kickoff-return touchdown. *Photo courtesy of Getty Images.*

been willing to let him go for a fourth-round draft pick. And a hamstring injury during training camp had kept Moss on the sideline during the preseason.

Welker was a talented return man who had been very successful playing against New England while he was with the Miami Dolphins. But there was no way to gauge his potential to succeed in a Patriots uniform.

What was known as Hobbs stepped out of the end zone was that the Pats had come out of the first half of their season's first game with a 14–7 lead. That was good. They had the ball to start the second half. That was promising. But there was Hobbs looking to manufacture something in an impossible situation—and likely sticking the offense with awful field position. That was horrifying.

**Ellis Hobbs lets the Giants Stadium crowd know exactly how it's going to be following his second-half opening kickoff-return TD.** *Photo courtesy of AP Images.*

Then the wedge cut left, and so did Hobbs. He appeared to still be in trouble as he cut across the hash marks at the 8-yard line with a trio of Jets right behind him. But he sped away from them and turned upfield just outside the left hash. Blocks by Troy Brown at the 12 and Benjamin Watson at the 15 opened a hole in the coverage, and Hobbs zipped through it. He skipped away from defensive end David Bowens, who dove at Hobbs' feet at the 20. And with one last key block by Heath Evans at the 33, Hobbs was set free. From there, he worked his way to the left sideline and flew up the field and into the end zone.

A play that started out looking like a major mistake had turned into the longest kickoff return in NFL history. The Jets never came close to challenging through the rest of the game. And the 2007 Patriots were officially off to the races.

# Game Details

**New England Patriots 38 • New York Jets 14**

| Patriots | 7 | 7 | 14 | 10 | **38** |
|---|---|---|---|---|---|
| Jets | 0 | 7 | 7 | 0 | **14** |

**Date:** September 9, 2007

**Team Records:** Patriots 1–0; Jets 0–1

**Scoring Plays:**

NE Welker 11-yard pass from Brady (Gostkowski PAT)

NYJ Coles 7-yard pass from Pennington (Nugent PAT)

NE Watson 5-yard pass from Brady (Gostkowski PAT)

NE Hobbs 108-yard kickoff return (Gostkowski PAT)

NE Moss 51-yard pass from Brady (Gostkowski PAT)

NYJ Coles 1-yard-pass from Pennington (Nugent PAT)

NE Gostkowski 22-yard FG

NE Evans 1-yard run (Gostkowski)

# That Randy Moss

Between the trips to New Jersey that bookended the Patriots' 2007 season, Randy Moss found his way onto the ESPN and NFL Films highlight reels on a near-weekly basis. He continued to make spectacular plays without Tom Brady in 2008. And even in 2009, though he was hampered by the lingering effects of a separated shoulder for the last 12 weeks of the regular season and the Pats' lone postseason game, Moss found ways to make a few eye-poppingly big plays. But the first time is always special, and Brady's first big touchdown pass to Moss endures as one of the most memorable moments of a record-setting season.

Leading 21–7 midway through the third quarter, the Pats faced second-and-six at their own 49-yard line. Moss lined up wide right but moved inside the numbers just prior to the snap. Brady took the snap from under center, sold a play-fake to Laurence Maroney, then dropped back to the 40 and held up a few seconds to give Moss time to run his route down and across the field. Brady stepped up to the 41 and fired deep left, where Moss was speeding along in triple coverage. There was nothing linebacker Jonathan Vilma, cornerback David Barrett, or safety Erik Coleman could do. Moss caught the pass in stride at the 2 and carried on into the end zone. It was a thing of beauty and the start of something even better.

**I**n any return, there's one guy who's not blocked. And your job as the return man is to make that guy miss. If you can do that, you've got a chance to take it all the way. Ellis came out of the end zone because he felt like he could make that guy miss.

—KEVIN FAULK

# Heartbreakers

September 9, 1960

# Truck Day

### The Patriots Surrender the AFL's First Punt-Return TD

The Boston Patriots weren't supposed to come out on the losing side of the American Football League's first game ever. As a matter of fact, it wasn't even supposed to be close.

The Denver Broncos rolled into town for the new league's inaugural match as 16-point underdogs. The Broncos had been clobbered by the Pats 43–6 in a pre-season game a little more than a month earlier. And no one had any reason to expect a substantially different result in the teams' first meeting that actually counted, particularly given the venue shift from the Broncos' preseason base in Pomona, California, to the Patriots' regular-season home, Boston University Field.

But if the Patriots' first four decades were destined to be colored by disappointment and heartbreak—by potential unrealized and triumph denied—fate apparently saw no reason to avoid getting right down to business. It selected Gene Mingo to deliver the bad news.

Returning punts wasn't Mingo's job going into the game. That was one of the roles filled by halfback Al Carmichael. But Carmichael, who caught the 59-yard touchdown pass from Frank Tripucka that put Denver up 7–3 in the second quarter, was hurt late in the half. So at halftime, Broncos coach Frank Filchock approached Mingo and told him he was adding punt returns to the rookie's regular duties, which included playing fullback and place kicking.

"It sort of freaked me out that during my first game I was going to have to do something I had never prepared for," Mingo remembers. "But in those days, football wasn't so specialized. We had 33 guys on that team. If you wanted to keep your job, you did what your coach asked."

Mingo did a bit more than anyone could have expected.

As the clock ticked away in the third quarter with neither offense accomplishing much—a fact at least partially attributable to poor lighting, which made passing the ball increasingly difficult as the night wore on—Mingo took a punt from Tom Greene at the Broncos' 24-yard line.

He started left, saw that he had good blocking to his right, and cut over to take advantage of it. Eluding coverage, Mingo charged up the right sideline leaving only Greene, the backup quarterback and punter, between him and the end zone.

Broncos great Gene Mingo helped get a 50-year trend started with his 76-yard punt-return touchdown in the AFL's first-ever game. *Photo courtesy of AP Images.*

# A Bad Matchup

Sometimes a team just has another team's number. That's surely been the case with the Broncos and the Patriots. No other team among the original eight AFL franchises has been as consistent a thorn in the Patriots' sides as have the Broncos. Through the 2009 season, the Broncos hold a 25–16 record against the Patriots; they're 2–0 against the Pats in the postseason and are the only team that has twice beaten New England in the playoffs. Even in the Belichick-Brady era, in which the Pats have reversed their fortunes against most of the teams that traditionally dogged them, things with Denver haven't changed. Bill Belichick's Patriots are 3–6 against the Broncos, a record that includes a 27–13 loss in the divisional round of the 2005–06 playoffs. The Patriots' previous postseason loss to Denver came in the 1986–87 playoffs when the AFC East champion Pats traveled to Denver to face a Super Bowl–bound Broncos squad in a game that would illustrate the differences between the two squads' class of '83 quarterbacks. Denver's John Elway threw a 48-yard touchdown pass to wideout Vance Johnson at the end of the third quarter that put his team ahead 20–17. New England's Tony Eason took a sack in the end zone with 1:37 remaining in the fourth period, sealing Denver's victory at 22–17. In 2009 the Broncos tied the Patriots 17–17 late in the fourth quarter, then won the game with a 41-yard field goal on the first possession of overtime.

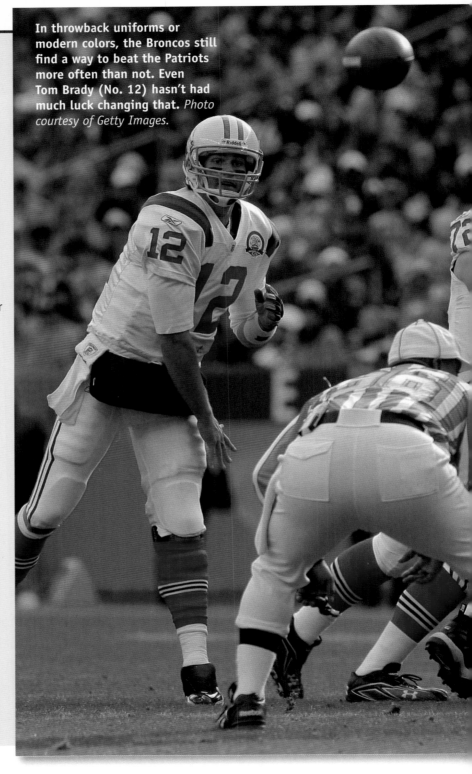

In throwback uniforms or modern colors, the Broncos still find a way to beat the Patriots more often than not. Even Tom Brady (No. 12) hasn't had much luck changing that. *Photo courtesy of Getty Images.*

"Not only did I punt the ball that Gene Mingo returned for the TD, I also was the last Patriot player to have a chance to tackle him," Greene recalls. "I tried, but he ran over me like a truck in what was surely a testimony to his determination and ability."

Mingo powered the full 76 yards down the field and into the end zone, logging the first punt-return touchdown in AFL history and posting the points that would decide the game. Although the Patriots would close the gap with a 10-yard touchdown pass from Butch Songin to Jim Colclough at the end of the third, it wouldn't be enough. A late interception of a Songin pass deep in Denver territory would seal the upset victory for the visitors.

Mingo's play didn't work out perfectly for Denver, though. Gassed from his long run, Mingo wasn't able to connect for the extra point.

"I was tired. I was shocked. My legs just turned to rubber," Mingo recalls. "I took the biggest divot, and the ball just went nowhere."

Cold comfort for the Patriots and their fans, of course. But that, too, can be taken now as a taste of what was on tap for the next 40 years or so.

# Game Details

**Boston Patriots 10 • Denver Broncos 13**

| | | | | | |
|---|---|---|---|---|---|
| **Patriots** | 3 | 0 | 7 | 0 | **10** |
| **Broncos** | 0 | 7 | 6 | 0 | **13** |

**Date:** September 9, 1960

**Team Records:** Patriots 0–1; Broncos 1–0

**Scoring Plays:**

BOS Cappelletti 35-yard FG

DEN Carmichael 59-yard pass from Tripucka (Mingo PAT)

DEN Mingo 76-yard punt return (kick failed)

BOS Colclough 10-yard pass from Songin (Cappelletti PAT)

December 20, 1964

# Throwing It All Away

Key Interception Costs the Patriots an AFL
Title Shot

The way it was supposed to work was that the Patriots were
going to get another shot at an AFL crown. And this time
they were going to win.

The Pats had been beaten badly by the San Diego Chargers in the 1963
championship. They'd overcome the Bills in Buffalo in a tiebreaker match
to decide the Eastern Division title only to travel west and have their heads
torn off 51–10 by Sid Gillman's team.

But 1964 was going to be different. The Chargers had taken the Western
Division, but they were limping into the postseason. They'd have to travel to
face the Eastern Division champs. The only question was whether it would
be Boston or Buffalo playing the ungracious host.

And it looked pretty certain that it would be Boston.

The Bills had a half-game lead on the Patriots in the standings, but
the Pats were riding a five-game winning streak (which included a 38–26
victory over the Bills in Buffalo). And the final game of the season, the game
that would decide the division, was to be played at Fenway Park.

The Patriots were confident. The fans were confident. The press was
confident. If it hadn't been for the snowstorm on the way, Boston might

**Babe Parilli joined the Patriots
in 1961 and led the offense
through 1967.** *Photo courtesy of
Getty Images.*

have rolled out the welcome mat for the Chargers a week early. In truth a lot of things might have been different if not for the storm.

On the morning of the game, players awoke to find the city already blanketed in snow. It was piled high and coming down furiously.

Gino Cappelletti, the Pats' wide receiver and place-kicker, remembers getting bogged down in traffic on Route 9 on his way to the park.

"I was actually late getting to the game," Cappelletti recalls. "The game was to kick off at 1:00, and I got there at 12:40. Fortunately, they pushed the game back to 2:00."

They did some other things, too. Like bringing in a helicopter to try to blow snow off the field, then covering the playing surface until just before game time. Still, within a few minutes of the tarpaulin being removed, the yard lines disappeared under newly fallen snow.

The game was played amid fierce winds and on difficult footing. The latter factor proved an ongoing problem for the Pats, whose stellar pass-rush was slowed, allowing Buffalo quarterback Jack Kemp the time he needed to pick apart Boston's secondary.

Kemp put the Bills up early with a 57-yard touchdown strike to Elbert Dubenion. And when the Patriots scored

One-time Patriots coach Lou Saban celebrates his Bills' AFL championship with Pete Gogolak, Jack Kemp, and Wray Carlton. *Photo courtesy of AP Images.*

# The Power of the Babe

Vito "Babe" Parilli was the fourth overall pick in the 1952 NFL draft, selected by the Green Bay Packers. He had been an outstanding college player under Paul "Bear" Bryant at the University of Kentucky, leading the Wildcats to victory over the No. 1–ranked Oklahoma Sooners in the 1951 Sugar Bowl and the Texas Christian University Horned Frogs in the 1952 Cotton Bowl. Parilli played decent ball for a pair of bad Green Bay squads, then spent a few years bouncing back and forth between the Packers, the Cleveland Browns, and the Canadian Football League's Ottawa Rough Riders. He spent the AFL's inaugural season as a member of the Oakland Raiders, playing behind Tom Flores. Traded to the Patriots in April 1961, Parilli took over starting duties from Butch Songin during his first season in Boston. And it was with the Patriots that he finally came into his own as a pro. Over his seven seasons with the Pats, Parilli amassed a record of

> **W**e threw some interceptions back then. We didn't do this nickel-and-dime stuff. We threw downfield. We were a vertical passing league. That's what we did.
>
> **—BABE PARILLI**

44–32–7. In 1964 he set a franchise record for passing touchdowns in a single season, 31, that stood until Tom Brady obliterated it in 2007. Parilli is considered perhaps the best field-goal holder in professional football history. His pairing with Gino Cappelletti was dubbed the "Grand Opera." Parilli ended his career with the New York Jets, who brought him in to mentor Joe Namath. He earned a ring and saw some time on the field as Namath's backup in Super Bowl III.

---

a touchdown of their own, coach Mike Holovak, hoping to avoid a tie that would have given the division crown to Buffalo, opted to go for two. The attempt failed.

"It was coming to me, and I slipped on a piece of ice in the end zone," Cappelletti says.

And so it continued to go. As the fourth quarter got under way, the Bills were ahead 17–6 and the Patriots' hopes of a championship rematch were fading. Driving, and badly in need of a score, Pats quarterback Babe Parilli tried to force a ball in to Jim Colclough at the Buffalo 45-yard line. Defensive back Charley Warner, playing zone coverage, cut off the pass, made a pick, and returned it to the Boston 17. Two plays later, Kemp found the end zone, and the game was effectively over.

Parilli puts the blame on himself: "It's not easy to throw the ball in weather like that, but I probably threw a lousy pass anyway."

Lousy pass? Lousy storm? Either way, it was lousy luck.

## Game Details

**Boston Patriots 14 • Buffalo Bills 24**

| | | | | | |
|---|---|---|---|---|---|
| **Patriots** | 6 | 0 | 0 | 8 | **14** |
| **Bills** | 7 | 10 | 0 | 7 | **24** |

**Date:** December 20, 1964

**Team Records:** Patriots 10-3-1; Bills 12-2

**Scoring Plays:**

BUF Dubenion 57-yard pass from Kemp (Gogolak PAT)

BOS Romeo 37-yard pass from Parilli (pass failed)

BUF Kemp 1-yard run (Gogolak PAT)

BUF Gogolak 12-yard FG

BUF Kemp 1-yard run (Gogolak PAT)

BOS Romeo 15-yard pass from Parilli (Colclough pass from Parilli)

Mike Haynes (No. 40) slips away from Gene Upshaw too late to stop Ken Stabler. Tim Fox (No. 48) and Steve Nelson (No. 57) also couldn't get to Stabler in time. *Photo courtesy of AP Images.*

# Snaked

## Ken Stabler's One-Yard TD Steals a Playoff Win from a Great Patriots Squad

In one regard, it was as simple as could be: Trailing 21–17 with 14 seconds to play, the Oakland Raiders lined up on second-and-goal at the New England 1-yard line. Raiders quarterback Ken Stabler took the snap, faked a pitchout, then rolled out left. Taking advantage of a perfectly executed block by guard Gene Upshaw that wiped Patriots cornerback Mike Haynes out of the play, Stabler lunged headlong into the end zone. Touchdown.

The extra point put the Raiders ahead 24–21 with only enough time left on the clock for the Patriots to try the kind of desperation pass that fails 99.9 percent of the time—including on this occasion. Oakland won the divisional-round playoff game and moved ahead on the path to its first Super Bowl victory.

New England went home empty-handed.

The play itself was pretty standard. Nothing fancy. Just enough to sneak past a stout Patriots defense and put up points when it mattered most. Simple.

Except for how it wasn't. And not just because the result decided the postseason fates of at least two teams.

The truth of the matter is that the Raiders should never have been in the position to run *any* goal-line play.

The game, and Oakland's season, should have ended something on the order of 40 seconds of game time earlier with a futile attempt by the Raiders to convert a fourth-and-18 from the Patriots' 28-yard line. Or, at least for one beautiful moment, that's what appeared to be on tap.

The Raiders, though they had finished the 1976 season with an NFL-best record of 13–1, were all but beaten. They'd put up a valiant effort to rally in the fourth quarter after falling behind 21–10. And they'd been given a chance to pull off a win when Patriots kicker John Smith couldn't quite get a 50-yard field-goal attempt over the goal post with four minutes left in the game.

But Oakland had fallen short. Needing a touchdown, they mounted an effective drive and marched steadily downfield all the way to the New England 20. But on first down with 1:24 to play, Patriots defensive end Mel Lunsford sacked Stabler for a loss of eight. Then, after a second-down incompletion, Stabler dropped back to pass only to have his throw deflected by Patriots tackle Ray "Sugar Bear" Hamilton.

It was going to be fourth-and-18. The Patriots, who had handed the Raiders their only loss of the regular season—a 48–17 shellacking at Foxborough's Schaefer Stadium in Week 4—were about to take it to Oakland yet again. The only question was whether the Pats would face Pittsburgh or Baltimore in the AFC Championship Game.

And then the yellow flag flew. Referee Ben Dreith called Hamilton for roughing the passer, saying Hamilton had delivered a blow to the quarterback's head after deflecting the pass.

# Game Details

## New England Patriots 21 • Oakland Raiders 24

| Patriots | 7 | 0 | 14 | 0 | 21 |
|---|---|---|---|---|---|
| Raiders | 3 | 7 | 0 | 14 | 24 |

**Date:** December 18, 1976

**Team Records:** Patriots 11–4; Raiders 14–1

**Scoring Plays:**

NE Johnson 1-yard run (Smith PAT)

OAK Mann 40-yard FG

OAK Biletnikoff 31-yard pass from Stabler (Mann PAT)

NE Francis 26-yard pass from Grogan (Smith PAT)

NE Phillips 3-yard run (Smith PAT)

OAK van Eeghen 1-yard run (Mann PAT)

OAK Stabler 1-yard run (Mann PAT)

No one who wasn't wearing silver and black (or black-and-white stripes) believed it then. And no one who doesn't bleed Raiders colors believes it now.

Hamilton's hand may have made some kind of contact with Stabler's helmet. But there was certainly no serious blow delivered. And Dreith's call has subsequently been rated among the worst in league history.

Good call or bad didn't matter during the game, however. All that mattered that day in Oakland was that Dreith's call advanced the ball to the Patriots' 13 and gave the Raiders a new set of downs.

Stabler and the Raiders took full advantage, moving the ball to the goal line for a final try.

The Patriots stopped running back Pete Banaszak on first down. On second, their luck ran out.

Haynes, the only New England defender who had a real shot at stopping Stabler before he reached the end zone, was neutralized by Upshaw in a classic clash of future Hall of Famers. Safety Tim Fox and linebacker Steve Nelson were both in the area, but neither had enough time to get to Stabler.

For the Raiders, it was exactly the right play at exactly the right time.

For the Patriots, it was a frustrating end for what remains—even in the Belichick-Brady era—one of the best squads in franchise history.

Nelson is one of many members of the 1976 Patriots who still hold that Dreith's call did them in. The call didn't directly put points on the board, but it did, Nelson says, take the wind out of New England's sails. The Patriots were talented but inexperienced. The reversal of a game-clinching defensive play, Nelson says, messed with players' heads at exactly the wrong moment.

"We played tactically such a good game up to then," Nelson says. "We were in a position to win with one more play. And then it was gone. Being a young team, you don't know how to handle adversity. We just weren't able to rebound from it."

# Bitter End

Fans remember the 1976 Patriots primarily as a team that was robbed by poor officiating. Ben Dreith's phantom roughing-the-passer flag against Ray Hamilton was hardly the only questionable call in the postseason loss to Oakland. There were non-calls—Raiders safety George Atkinson got away with an elbow to the face that broke Pats tight end Russ Francis' nose; Francis was also the victim of blatant pass interference by linebacker Phil Villapiano that officials somehow failed to notice—and an assortment of holding calls against New England in which apparently only the officials were able to see the infractions.

But it's important also to remember that Patriots squad as a straight-out great football team. Its roster included John Hannah, arguably the best offensive lineman ever to play the game; Mike Haynes, easily the best cornerback in the league at that time; and an assortment of standout players on both sides of the ball—from Francis, Sam Cunningham, Steve Grogan, and Leon Gray on offense to Steve Nelson, Tim Fox, Hamilton, and Julius Adams on *D*. The 1976 Patriots also were expertly coached by Chuck Fairbanks and a staff of assistants whose influence on the pro game continues to be felt. Fairbanks' coaching staff included Hank Bullough, who brought the 3-4 defense to the NFL; Ron Erhardt and Ray Perkins, whose offensive system teams—including the Patriots—still run; Red Miller; and Raymond Berry.

It was a team that not only could have, but probably should have, won it all.

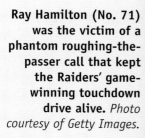

**Ray Hamilton (No. 71) was the victim of a phantom roughing-the-passer call that kept the Raiders' game-winning touchdown drive alive.** *Photo courtesy of Getty Images.*

January 26, 1986

# It's a Pumpkin

Refrigerator Perry's Touchdown Run Visits
Midnight upon a Cinderella Season

The 1985 Patriots' glass slipper didn't fall off. It was
knocked off. Then shattered. Publicly and painfully.
And it was a 308-pound defensive tackle, wearing his
trademark ear-to-ear smile, who delivered the final
stomp.

The end of Super Bowl XX's third quarter was approaching with
the Chicago Bears leading an increasingly exhausted New England
Patriots squad 37–3.

The Bears, who had steamrolled their way through the '85 regular
season and the NFC playoffs, were at it again, pummeling a Patriots
team that was good but nowhere near good enough. The game was
over, but Chicago wasn't finished. Looking at first-and-goal from the
1-yard line, Bears coach Mike Ditka sent his rookie defensive tackle,
William "the Refrigerator" Perry, onto the field to line up at fullback.
While Pats fans buried their heads, viewers everywhere else perked up.
Everyone knew exactly what was coming. They'd seen it before; they'd
been waiting to see it again.

Perry was an unusual sports celebrity. Under a lot of circumstances,
he might have gone largely unnoticed, perhaps through an entire career.
But Perry's circumstances didn't even approach the typical.

Refrigerator Perry scores the Super Bowl rushing touchdown that many in New England and Chicago believed should have been Walter Payton's. *Photo courtesy of Getty Images.*

**The Fridge's spike was about more than his TD. It was the start of the Bears' victory celebration.** *Photo courtesy of Getty Images.*

**E**verybody knew they were probably going to do it in that game. He was a big man, and people enjoyed seeing him with the ball. I don't think it was meant as a slap in the face to us.

—STEVE NELSON

Enormous for his era, Perry first made news when he was labeled a waste of a first-round draft pick by Chicago's temperamental defensive coordinator Buddy Ryan.

The assessment itself didn't much matter. The 1985 Bears were a historically good team; one young lineman was never going to make a significant difference either way. But it ensured that Perry would be watched all season long.

And as the Bears progressed through the season to a 15–1 finish then shut out both of their conference play-offs opponents, Perry became famous not so much for his contributions at his natural position as for his size, his unerring good nature off the field, and his contributions to the offense. Lining up at fullback, Perry scored three times during the season. Football fans enjoyed seeing it, and they wanted to see it again in the Super Bowl.

Of course, that might not have happened had the game been closer. You don't call plays for their entertainment value with a championship on the line.

But the Bears and Ditka never had to worry much about that. Sure, the Patriots went into Super Bowl XX on an amazing roll. Playing their first full season under head coach Raymond Berry, they fought back from a 2–3 start to finish the season 11–5. They became the first team in NFL history to reach the Super Bowl by way of three straight postseason road victories. And they scored the fastest points in Super Bowl history when kicker Tony Franklin put up a field goal 1:19 into the first quarter. But the Patriots—though they were tough, talented, and determined—were never on the same level as the Bears.

By the time the second half rolled around, the Bears were toying with the Pats. So Perry got his turn in the end zone.

Joining the offense on the field, Perry lined up five yards behind the line of scrimmage. Taking the handoff from quarterback Jim McMahon, Perry barreled up the gut, over a spent New England defensive line, and into the end zone. Simple.

With the extra point, the play put the Bears ahead 44–3 in a game they would win 46–10.

And while the play call struck many Pats fans as an insult, for members of the team the TD was simply a matter of course, a return from high-flying hopes to brutal reality.

## Game Details

### New England Patriots 10 • Chicago Bears 46

| Patriots | 3 | 0 | 0 | 7 | 10 |
|----------|---|----|----|---|----|
| Bears | 13 | 10 | 21 | 2 | 46 |

**Date:** January 26, 1986

**Team Records:** Patriots 14–6; Bears 18–1

**Scoring Plays:**

NE Franklin 36-yard FG

CHI Butler 28-yard FG

CHI Butler 24-yard FG

CHI Suhey 11-yard run (Butler PAT)

CHI McMahon 2-yard run (Butler PAT)

CHI Butler 24-yard FG

CHI McMahon 1-yard run (Butler PAT)

CHI Phillips 28-yard INT return (Butler PAT)

CHI Perry 1-yard run (Butler PAT)

NE Fryar 8-yard pass from Grogan (Franklin PAT)

CHI Safety, Grogan sacked in end zone by Waechter

## No Escaping It

If there's anything positive to be said about a team taking an absolute pounding in the Super Bowl, it has to be that at least the result doesn't leave any questions unanswered. The '85 Pats weren't champions, but they were a team that went exactly as far as they could. As coach Raymond Berry sees it, the equation was simple: "We were a first-grade offense meeting a PhD defense in that game, and there wasn't too much we could do about it." Berry doesn't offer that by way of an apology. The coach had taken over the team in the middle of the 1984 season after Ron Meyer was fired; he installed his offense during the 1985 preseason, and he kept it simple on purpose. "We had great players," he says. "And the only way you can screw up great players is by asking too much of them." A simple offense, in combination with a solid defense, was enough to get the Pats to their first Super Bowl. And in some seasons, it might have been enough to deliver a Lombardi Trophy. But not against the '85 Bears. "The Chicago Bears defense was one of the top three I ever came up against either playing or coaching," says Berry, whose Hall of Fame career as a wide receiver spanned 13 seasons. Some team was going to lose to the Bears in the Super Bowl. There's no shame in it having been the Patriots.

I've heard a few comments from time to time that it was an insult to us. I didn't really pay all that much attention to it. The Bears were having fun at that stage of the game.

—RAYMOND BERRY

January 26, 1997

# Somebody Stop Him

Desmond Howard Goes End-to-End in Super Bowl XXXI

Larry McCarren was taken aback.

Working as a radio game analyst in Green Bay, the former Packer had watched his team tear through the 1996 season. He knew exactly how good the Packers were. And although he respected the AFC champion Patriots, he never expected Super Bowl XXXI to be truly competitive.

"The Packers were favored by quite a lot," McCarren recalls (it was 14 points, to be exact). "And I knew they were a hell of a team. So the fact that it was going back and forth for so long really surprised me."

It really surprised a lot of people. Virtually no one outside of New England— and relatively few honest fans at home—gave the Patriots much of a chance in their second-ever Super Bowl appearance.

Green Bay was just one of those teams: Best in the league from Week 1 through Week 17. They finished the regular season with the NFL's top-ranked offense *and* defense, an accomplishment that's beyond rare (the only other team ever to pull it off was the unde-feated 1972 Miami Dolphins). The Packers beat their regular-season opponents by an average of better than 15 points. They were even more dominant in the playoffs.

The Packers had Reggie White, one of the best defensive ends to ever play the game. And they had Brett Favre, who had been named league MVP for the second year running. They were considered a team of destiny.

The Patriots were just a team. A good team. Not a lucky team. Not even a team like the 1985 squad that had willed its way to Super Bowl XX. A team with a high-powered offense and a better-than-average *D*. A team that had won 11 regular-season games and allowed its two conference playoffs opponents nine points combined.

The Pats had Drew Bledsoe, who was having one of his best seasons. They had an outstanding running back in Curtis Martin.

And, at least for the moment, they had Bill Parcells running the show.

That was all nice. But no one figured it would be enough.

So, yeah, McCarren was anything but alone in his shock when, late in the third quarter, the Patriots pulled to within six points. Martin's 18-yard touchdown run created the impression that the game might well go down to the wire.

Then a Desmond Howard kickoff return pulled the rug out from under New England.

It didn't initially appear Green Bay's talented return man would get much of an opportunity. Adam Vinatieri's high, floating kick backed Howard up to the goal line and gave the Patriots time to get downfield. Howard, though, managed to find a seam. He eluded a lunge by linebacker Marty Moore at the Patriots' 20-yard line. Two steps later, he slipped from the grasp of wide receiver Hason Graham, who was playing in place of an injured Troy Brown. And from there, Howard poured on the speed, leaving a few Patriots to pursue him hopelessly the other 75 yards to the end zone.

It was the longest kickoff return TD in Super Bowl history. It helped Howard earn MVP honors, and it sucked every last bit of wind out of the Patriots' sails.

"After that, the defense was really able to tee off," McCarren points out. "It changed the complexion of the game from one that was doable for the Patriots to one that wasn't."

And when the game ended with Green Bay in front 35–21, no one, least of all McCarren, was in any way surprised.

**The Patriots had momentum at that point in the game, and that return took every bit of that momentum away.**

**—GIL SANTOS**

## Game Details

**New England Patriots 21 • Green Bay Packers 35**

| | | | | | |
|---|---|---|---|---|---|
| **Patriots** | 14 | 0 | 7 | 0 | **21** |
| **Packers** | 10 | 17 | 8 | 0 | **35** |

**Date:** January 26, 1997

**Team Records:** Patriots 13–6; Packers 16–3

**Scoring Plays:**

GB Rison 54-yard pass from Favre (Jacke PAT)
GB Jacke 37-yard FG
NE Byars 1-yard pass from Bledsoe (Vinatieri PAT)
NE Coates 4-yard pass from Bledsoe (Vinatieri PAT)
GB Freeman 81-yard pass from Favre (Jacke PAT)
GB Jacke 31-yard FG
GB Favre 2-yard run (Jacke PAT)
NE Martin 18-yard run (Vinatieri PAT)
GB Howard 99-yard kickoff return (Chmura pass from Favre)

**Given enough time, the best team usually finds a way to win.**

**—LARRY MCCARREN, GREEN BAY PACKERS RADIO ANALYST**

# The Tuna Checks In and Checks Out

Chances are, the Patriots weren't beating the Green Bay Packers in Super Bowl XXXI one way or the other. For the second time, a Patriots team had come on at exactly the wrong time. The Packers were one of those rare teams that are just far too good to be denied a championship. Still, it might have been nice if the Patriots' head coach had been fully engaged.

Bill Parcells had been brought to New England four years earlier to bring respectability to a franchise that had fallen into a serious state of disrepair. He'd accomplished some of that simply by walking through the door, taken it a step further by bringing in Drew Bledsoe, and reached a major milestone by not only ending a streak of five straight losing seasons but getting the Patriots into the playoffs in 1994.

But when it came time to ready his squad for the Super Bowl, Parcells had a higher priority: himself. The coach, whose relationship with team owner Robert Kraft was strained, to say the least, spent a chunk of the week before Super Bowl XXXI making arrangements to leave New England and take over as coach of the New York Jets. And after word of what was happening leaked to the *Boston Globe*, he spent even more time denying the truth. His denials ended after the game, though. While his team flew back to Boston, second-best, Parcells went directly to New Jersey to meet with his new employers.

**Bill Parcells revived the Patriots in 1993 and let them down at the exact wrong moment four seasons later.** *Photo courtesy of AP Images.*

October 31, 2004

# Killing Blow

## Halloween Massacre Pick Sets Up an End to a Historic Winning Streak

It wasn't like anyone thought the Patriots were never going to lose again.

Streaks invariably get snapped. And no team had ever put together a winning streak like the one the Patriots carried from Week 5 of the 2003 season through Week 7 of 2004: 21 games without a loss. That's 18 regular-season contests, two conference playoff games, and a Super Bowl. No team had ever done anything like it. And chances are, it'll be a very long time before any team comes close. (While the Pats' record run of 18 regular-season wins fell five years later to the Indianapolis Colts, the real mark is the virtually unapproachable one that includes the league championship.)

And the truth of the matter was that there was plenty of reason to suspect the streak might end in Pittsburgh well before the Patriots and Steelers ever took the field on Halloween.

Forget that Pittsburgh had a rookie starting under center. Ben Roethlisberger was playing well enough not to lose games. And the Steelers defense was doing a more than ample job of ensuring opponents didn't win.

The Pats were undefeated through their first six games; the Steelers had a single loss. But the Pats were hurting. Corey Dillon missed the game with a thigh injury. Cornerback Tyrone Poole missed his second straight with a knee. The Patriots had fought through injuries and adversity to win a lot of games during their streak, but there had to be an end point.

And it didn't take long for the odds against the Pats to get even worse. Midway through the first quarter, the team's best cornerback, Ty Law, was lost with a broken bone in his left foot. The injury would end not only Law's season but his Patriots career.

Two plays after Law went out, his replacement, rookie Randall Gay, was torched on a 47-yard touchdown pass from Roethlisberger to Plaxico Burress.

It was neither Law's absence nor Gay's play that cost the Patriots the game, though. It was turnovers.

The Patriots gave the ball away four times. Tom Brady fumbled once and threw a pair of picks, and the usually reliable Kevin Faulk also lost a fumble. And on each occasion, the Steelers converted the Pats' mistake into points.

Deshea Townsend turns upfield with an intercepted ball. His first-quarter pick six signaled an end to the Patriots' long winning streak. *Photo courtesy of AP Images.*

Tom Brady's second pick in the Halloween Massacre went to Ike Taylor. *Photo courtesy of AP Images.*

The worst of it came early. And quick.

Brady lost the ball on consecutive plays in the first quarter. With the Pats trailing 7–3 after the Burress touchdown, he coughed up the ball at the Patriots' 27-yard line. It took the Steelers five plays to find the end zone.

A kickoff later, with 67 yards between New England and a score and the game already feeling like it was slipping away, Brady dropped back looking to make something happen.

He threw for Bethel Johnson at the Steelers' 39, but the receiver fell down on the play. Pittsburgh cornerback Deshea Townsend snagged Brady's pass and sailed unchallenged up the right side of the field and into the end zone. The Pats were down 21–3. The first quarter wasn't quite over, but the game pretty clearly was.

# Game Details

### New England Patriots 20 • Pittsburgh Steelers 34

| Patriots | 3 | 7 | 3 | 7 | **20** |
|----------|----|----|----|----|--------|
| Steelers | 21 | 3 | 10 | 0 | **34** |

**Date:** October 31, 2004

**Team Records:** Patriots 6–1; Steelers 6–1

**Scoring Plays:**

NE Vinatieri 43-yard FG

PIT Burress 47-yard pass from Roethlisberger (Reed PAT)

PIT Burress 4-yard pass from Roethlisberger (Reed PAT)

PIT Townsend 39-yard INT return (Reed PAT)

PIT Reed 19-yard FG

NE Givens 2-yard pass from Brady (Vinatieri PAT)

PIT Bettis 2-yard run (Reed PAT)

NE Vinatieri 25-yard FG

PIT Reed 29-yard FG

NE Givens 23-yard pass from Brady (Vinatieri PAT)

The Steelers never looked back. They didn't need to. The Patriots would close the gap a bit during the final three quarters, but Brady's second pick, early in the second, and Faulk's fumble at the start of the third, ensured that the Pats never even got close to making it a game.

Every winning steak ends. Every fan knows it. But that didn't make the loss in Pittsburgh one bit easier to take.

# Piling Up Wins

With the exception of the moment Adam Vinatieri's game-winning kick cleared the crossbar on the final play of Super Bowl XXXVI, there's never been a better time to be a Patriots fan than during the team's historic winning streak. There's probably nothing more a football fan can possibly hope for than a year—392 days, actually—in which you never have to wonder what went wrong or how your team will turn things around. Not every win was on the level of a Super Bowl championship, of course. Nor were they all pretty. But more than a few were memorable.

Some are covered in detail elsewhere in this book. A few others:

On November 3, 2003, on *Monday Night Football*, Tom Brady hit David Givens for an 18-yard touchdown with 30 seconds remaining to lift the Pats to a 30–26 win over the Denver Broncos.

On November 23, 2003, the Pats came within 40 seconds of having to settle for a tie with the Houston Texans before Adam Vinatieri kicked a game winner in OT.

On December 27, 2003, the Pats drove home the extent to which they'd turned their season around, beating Buffalo 31–0, the same score by which they'd lost to the Bills in Week 1.

On January 10, 2004, the Patriots stopped the Tennessee Titans on fourth-and-12 at the New England 42-yard line with 1:38 remaining to secure a 17–14 divisional-round playoff victory.

Tom Brady's ill-advised throw to Troy Brown is cut off in the end zone by Broncos cornerback Champ Bailey. *Photo courtesy of Getty Images.*

January 14, 2006

# Like All Good Things

End-Zone Pick Helps End New England's 10-Game Playoff Winning Streak

It had to happen eventually, if only as a function of how professional football works. Sooner or later, there was going to be a postseason game in which the Patriots of Bill Belichick and Tom Brady would come up short. And, in a way, the only thing that ever called into question whether it would happen in the 2005–06 playoffs was the uncertainty surrounding whether the Pats would actually qualify for the postseason.

Still, the way it happened, with the Patriots surrendering five turnovers that led to 24 points for the Denver Broncos, was more than a bit of a shock. The Pats hadn't played flawless football during the league-record 10-game playoffs winning streak leading up to their divisional-round match in Denver, but they'd always managed to come up big when it mattered. Brady, in particular, had been a rock in the postseason, willing his team to victory at times and always making the right decisions with a game on the line.

A loss in the playoffs may have been inevitable, but a defeat effectively sealed by poor decision-making on Brady's part was nearly unthinkable. And that made it all the more heartbreaking.

The 2005 Patriots were probably a better team than they had any business being. Though the team entered the season as repeat champions—their dynasty established, their place in NFL history assured—they also came in as a team in flux. Charlie Weis and Romeo Crennel, who had run the offense and defense through all three championship seasons, had left the team for head-coaching jobs following Super Bowl XXXIX. The defense was short Ty Law, who was released in a salary cap–related move, and Ted Johnson, who surprised the team with a decision to retire on the eve of training camp. The offensive line had lost Joe Andruzzi and the receiving corps David Patten, both of whom left as free agents. And there was an on-field leadership void caused by Tedy Bruschi's absence for the first half of the season, after he suffered a stroke shortly after Super Bowl XXXIX, and Rodney Harrison, who was lost to injury in Week 3.

The Patriots played through the challenges, but they were an uneven squad. And by the time they fell to 4–4 with a 40–21 loss to the Indianapolis Colts in

Foxborough, almost no one was still dreaming of an NFL-first three-peat.

Still, they fought their way to 10–6 and handed the 12–4 Jacksonville Jaguars a 28–3 loss in the divisional round. That left a little bit of hope.

And there was hope still in the final minute of the third quarter in Denver.

## Making the Effort

To everyone watching the game, the effort Benjamin Watson made to catch Champ Bailey just short of the New England end zone was nothing short of amazing. Watson was on the other side of the field when Bailey grabbed Tom Brady's ill-advised pass in the Denver end zone. But the tight end still managed to hit Bailey at the Pats' goal line, knocking the ball out of Bailey's hands.

Watson attributes the play to a lesson he learned playing for Mark Richt at the University of Georgia. "When I was in college, I remember we were playing Clemson at home in Athens, and our running back fumbled the ball," Watson says. "One of the defensive backs picked it up and ran it in for a touchdown. And none of us on offense really chased him because we didn't think we could catch him. We still won the game, but the next week in practice, Coach Richt had some words for us about never giving up.

"That was something that we didn't forget," he says. "So we decided after that, if somebody picks the ball up, we're going to chase him no matter what, because we owe it to each other. We owe it to our teammates."

Watson carried that lesson to his pro career. He's careful to note, though, that he wasn't the only Patriot who pursued Bailey: "If you look at the film, everybody on offense was chasing him; I was just the one who caught him."

Despite two costly fumbles, the Pats were only down 10–6. And Brady had moved his team from their own 22-yard line to the Denver 5.

Then on third-and-goal, Brady tried to force the ball in to his go-to guy, Troy Brown, in the end zone, failing to take into account that the Broncos' outstanding cornerback Champ Bailey was covering Brown tightly.

Brown never had a shot at the ball. Bailey stepped in front of the pass, grabbed the ball, and took off down the left sideline. And while a heroic effort by Benjamin Watson kept Bailey out of the New England end zone, it only took the Broncos' offense one snap to score the touchdown that put the game away.

An unheard-of muffed punt by Brown that led to seven more Denver points in the fourth only made the message clearer: Nothing, but nothing, lasts forever.

## Game Details

### New England Patriots 13 • Denver Broncos 27

| | | | | | |
|---|---|---|---|---|---|
| **Patriots** | 0 | 3 | 3 | 7 | **13** |
| **Broncos** | 0 | 10 | 7 | 10 | **27** |

**Date:** January 14, 2006

**Team Records:** Patriots 11–7; Broncos 14–3

**Scoring Plays:**

NE Vinatieri 40-yard FG

DEN Anderson 1-yard run (Elam PAT)

DEN Elam 50-yard FG

NE Vinatieri 32-yard FG

DEN Anderson 1-yard run (Elam PAT)

DEN Smith 4-yard pass from Plummer (Elam PAT)

NE Givens 4-yard pass from Brady (Vinatieri PAT)

DEN Elam 34-yard FG

**Benjamin Watson raced 99 yards and across the field to knock the ball out of Champ Bailey's hands at the Patriots' goal line.** *Photo courtesy of AP Images.*

The first of Reche Caldwell's two big drops in the AFC Championship Game wasn't the most egregious. *Photo courtesy of AP Images.*

January 21, 2007

# Ping Ping Ping Ricochet Caldwell

Receiver's Buckneresque Miscue Proves Costly in AFC Championship Meltdown

Reche Caldwell didn't single-handedly lose the 2006–07 AFC Championship Game.

It's at least worth trying to keep that in mind. No matter how tempting it might be to heap the blame on one guy, it was an all-out collapse—not a single dropped pass, not even the second awful drop in one gigantic game by the same receiver—that denied the Patriots a chance to capture a fourth Super Bowl title in six years. (Well, an all-out collapse *and* a Colts team with a penchant for second-half heroics, and, you know, some really horrible officiating.)

Still, Caldwell did blow an opportunity to throw a big hurdle in the Colts' path.

Midway through the fourth quarter with the game tied at 28 and the Pats, who had led 21–6 at halftime, needing badly to find a way to stop the bleeding, Tom Brady brought his offense to the line on first-and-15 at the Indianapolis 18-yard line. Just before the snap, Caldwell, who had somehow been left uncovered on the right side of the field, signaled wildly to his quarterback.

Brady took the snap and delivered a quick pass to Caldwell, who remained not only wide open, but with a clear path to the end zone. He should have caught the ball, scored the touchdown, and let the Colts know that no matter how hard they tried, the Patriots would have a little more—just like always.

But that didn't happen. What did happen was that Caldwell dropped the ball. Not "couldn't catch the ball." *Dropped* it.

For the second time in the half, a ball that might as well have been handed to the receiver for all the work he needed to do to catch it bounced off his hands. The first time, when Caldwell dropped a pass in the end zone late in the third quarter, Jabar Gaffney was there on the next play to bail him out. This time, no such luck. And although it's true that Caldwell was flat-out mugged in the end zone two plays later (there was no flag), it hardly matters. The Pats should have scored seven. Instead, they had to settle for three.

And when all was said and done, the Colts had won by four.

At the very least, the touchdown Caldwell should have scored would have forced overtime. But it might also have taken some pressure off Brady, who might not have thrown the pick that sealed the loss while trying to drive for a touchdown in the final 50 seconds. Or it might have taken the wind out of Indy's sails.

So, yes, New England's defense, which had always held before, fell apart in the second half. Yes, Brady made mistakes. And, yes, the officials called a phantom pass-interference penalty on Ellis Hobbs in the end zone, setting up an easy touchdown for the Colts.

All of those factors contributed to the Patriots' loss. You have to remember that.

But it's true, all the same, that Caldwell's failure to execute fundamental skills put his team at a disadvantage in the second-biggest game a professional football team can play.

Caldwell is a wide receiver. His job is to catch the ball, which ought to be easy when it's thrown right to him and there's no one around to stop him. Fail to do that, and you've got a problem. Fail to do it twice in a huge game, and you've got more than a problem. You've got yourself a Bill Buckner situation. And no one wants to be Bill Buckner. Or Reche Caldwell.

> **T**o this day, Colts coaches and players will tell you, beating the Patriots in that game was a bigger deal than actually winning the Super Bowl two weeks later against Chicago.
>
> —BOB KRAVITZ,
> *INDIANAPOLIS STAR* SPORTS COLUMNIST

# Game Details

### New England Patriots 34 • Indianapolis Colts 38

| Patriots | 7 | 14 | 7 | 6 | **34** |
|---|---|---|---|---|---|
| Colts | 3 | 3 | 15 | 17 | **38** |

**Date:** January 21, 2007

**Team Records:** Patriots 14–5; Colts 15–4

**Scoring Plays:**

NE Mankins fumble recovery in end zone (Gostkowski PAT)

IND Vinatieri 42-yard FG

NE Dillon 7-yard run (Gostkowski PAT)

NE Samuel 39-yard INT return (Gostkowski PAT)

IND Vinatieri 26-yard FG

IND Manning 1-yard run (Vinatieri PAT)

IND Klecko 1-yard pass from Manning (Harrison pass from Manning)

NE Gaffney 6-yard pass from Brady (Gostkowski PAT)

IND Saturday fumble recovery in end zone (Vinatieri PAT)

NE Gostkowski 28-yard FG

IND Vinatieri 36-yard FG

NE Gostkowski 43-yard FG

IND Addai 3-yard run (Vinatieri PAT)

# Oops, Sorry

To begin with, there's no such thing as face-guarding in the NFL. Phil Simms, who was in the CBS booth for the 2006–07 AFC Championship Game, led a lot of viewers down the wrong path by explaining that Patriots cornerback Ellis Hobbs had been called for face-guarding. It was an understandable error. Hobbs was flagged for pass interference on a play in which he had made no contact with Colts wide receiver Reggie Wayne. There had to be some reason. And since Hobbs had put his hand up as the pass came down, Simms, perhaps channeling his inner college football analyst, figured face-guarding. Simms was also probably caught up in the energy of the game. The Colts, who had trailed by as much as 18 points in the first half, were nearing the end of a third-quarter drive with the potential to tie the score at 21. That's exciting. So maybe it just didn't occur to Simms to say that the officials had made a terrible call. And a costly one for the Patriots. Instead of facing third-and-seven at the 19, the Colts were awarded a first down at the goal line. It took one snap to get the ball into the end zone. The Colts maintained momentum and went on to win the conference title. And by the time Hobbs received a letter of apology from the league in the off-season, admitting that the call was incorrect, there wasn't anything anyone could have done to right the wrong.

**The officials made a bad pass-interference call against Ellis Hobbs, and Phil Simms confused the issue by labeling the infraction "face guarding."** *Photo courtesy of AP Images.*

February 3, 2008

# Are You Kidding?

The Most Spectacular Catch in Super Bowl History Dooms the Hope of 19–0

Nobody makes the kind of catch David Tyree made. Not in the Super Bowl. Not in the preseason. Not if there were a football version of the Harlem Globetrotters. Not ever.

Except for, you know, just the once. And at exactly the wrong time. Which is the thing that makes the whole deal completely horrible.

Because it's maybe the most amazing thing anyone's ever seen in the Super Bowl. Third-and-five at the New York Giants' 44-yard line with 1:15 left in the game and the Pats ahead 14–10. Eli Manning took the snap out of the shotgun and dropped back to the 37, where he quickly found himself in all kinds of trouble. For a fraction of a second, it appeared Richard Seymour and Jarvis Green were going to drop Manning for a big loss, leaving the Giants with no choice but to try to pick up a fourth-and-long. The game should have been over.

But Manning somehow escaped, rolled out to his right, scrambled to the 34, and, with Mike Vrabel bearing down on him, launched the ball to Tyree, who was in the middle of the field at the New England 24. And this, of course, is where it got truly astonishing. Because the ball was thrown high, nearly out of reach, but Tyree leapt, extended, and somehow managed to snag the ball with his right hand and press it up against his helmet, bringing his left hand in to help as he was dragged downward by Rodney Harrison. He held on to a ball no one could hope to hold on to. And in the process, he moved his team into position for the go-ahead touchdown.

Nobody makes that catch. Especially not a career special teamer who's never logged more than 19 receptions in a season and who managed exactly four catches in all of 2007. Especially not a guy who had already had his big moment in the Super Bowl, catching a five-yard touchdown pass early in the fourth quarter to put the Giants up 10–7.

Nobody makes that catch. Not when the Giants have their backs against the wall thanks to a clock-killing 80-yard touchdown drive that put the Pats on top 14–10 with 2:45 to play. Not when the Patriots are fighting to become the second team in NFL history to record a perfect season and the only team to do it since the expansion of the regular season to 16 games.

David Tyree's circus catch in Super Bowl XLII probably always will be remembered as one of the all-time great moments— but not by Patriots fans. *Photo courtesy of Getty Images.*

Eli Manning's improbable escape from a heavy Patriots pass rush set up the spectacular catch by David Tyree. *Photo courtesy of AP Images.*

Nobody makes that catch when Rodney Harrison—the toughest, hardest-hitting, most punishing, most determined safety in the league—is there to make sure the ball doesn't get caught.

It just doesn't happen.

Only, it did.

Tyree held on in spite of all the factors—physical and intangible alike—stacked up against him. It's at the same time the most spectacular, most athletic, and just plain luckiest grab in Super Bowl history.

And four plays later, Manning hit Plaxico Burress for a 13-yard touchdown. The Giants went ahead 17–14, leaving the Patriots with 29 seconds to try to make something happen. A few desperation passes later, the game was over. The dream of 19–0 was transformed into the nightmare of 18–1.

"It was a long time before I was able to watch that play again," says Gil Santos, a man who has witnessed just about every form of heartbreak imaginable as the Patriots' radio play-by-play announcer over the better part of four decades. "It's still upsetting. That play never should have happened. They should have had Manning sacked."

As Santos points out, though, there were ample opportunities for the Patriots to change the course of that game.

Indeed, there were at least four on the touchdown drive alone, not counting the pass to Tyree that shouldn't have been thrown *or* caught. There was the fourth-and-one when the Pats failed to prevent Brandon Jacobs from picking up a first down, the almost certain interception that somehow shot through Asante Samuel's hands on the sideline, the third-and-11 from the New England 25 that the Giants converted with a Manning pass to Steve Smith, and the go-ahead touchdown play on which 5'9" cornerback Ellis Hobbs was left alone to cover 6'5" wide receiver Burress.

There are lots of reasons 19–0 slipped away.

But it's still impossible to think about Super Bowl XLII without reliving Manning's escape and Tyree's catch. No matter how badly you might want to.

# Game Details

**New England Patriots 14 • New York Giants 17**

| | | | | | |
|---|---|---|---|---|---|
| **Patriots** | 0 | 7 | 0 | 7 | **14** |
| **Giants** | 3 | 0 | 0 | 14 | **17** |

**Date:** February 3, 2008

**Team Records:** Patriots 18–1; Giants 14–6

**Scoring Plays:**

NYG Tynes 32-yard FG

NE Maroney 1-yard run (Gostkowski PAT)

NYG Tyree 5-yard pass from Manning (Tynes PAT)

NE Moss 6-yard pass from Brady (Gostkowski PAT)

NYG Burress 13-yard pass from Manning (Tynes PAT)

## Suffering Through Spygate

Nothing, obviously, could possibly have so thoroughly darkened the memory of the Patriots' amazing 2007 season as the outcome of Super Bowl XLII. But Spygate—or, rather, the attention it got in the media—certainly didn't make it easier to appreciate the 16–0 run. From the moment the first story broke about a Patriots employee being stopped while videotaping New York Jets defensive signals from the sideline during the season-opening game, straight through to Super Bowl week (and beyond), the chatter was constant. And whether it was Jimmy Johnson asserting taping signals was neither new nor unusual, the *New York Post* affixing an asterisk to the Patriots' win-loss record, or the *Boston Herald* engaging in speculative reporting about a former Pats staffer who supposedly had a tape of the St. Louis Rams made in advance of Super Bowl XXXVI (a claim later proven false), the noise made it difficult at times to focus on just what an incredible team the Patriots had assembled. There was really nothing to Spygate. The Patriots' only real infraction was to ignore a league memo about where cameras could be positioned during games. Filming an opponent, including the team's defensive signals, was entirely legal. The Pats never cheated, but the talk revolved around whether they did. And so an act of illegal camera placement that was shut down in the first quarter of the season's first game provided a constant source of distraction—for fans and the media, though clearly not the team—during an otherwise spectacular season.

**T**hat was the greatest play in Super Bowl history. It's just too bad the Patriots were on the wrong side of it.

—GIL SANTOS

Colts cornerback Melvin Bullitt tackles Kevin Faulk on fourth down. Officials ruled Faulk was just short of a first down. *Photo courtesy of AP Images.*

November 15, 2009

# It Just Doesn't Matter

## Fourth-and-Two Call Illustrates That Not Every Big Play Is a Big Play

At the time, it seemed like a big deal.

With his team leading the Indianapolis Colts 34–28 and the two-minute warning approaching, Bill Belichick opted to go for it on fourth-and-two from his own 28-yard line rather than punt and turn the ball over to Indy's potent offense.

Tom Brady lined up in the shotgun, took the snap, and threw a quick swing pass to Kevin Faulk, who caught the ball just across the 30. Faulk was hit immediately and carried backward by Colts defensive back Melvin Bullitt. And while it appeared for all the world that the Patriots had picked up the first down, the officials didn't award Faulk forward progress. They spotted the ball short of the marker. The Pats turned the ball over on downs.

Four plays later, the Colts scored the go-ahead touchdown, leaving just 16 seconds on the clock. The Pats couldn't do anything with the time. And so the Colts, who had trailed 34–21 with two and half minutes left in the game, recorded a come-from-behind victory over the Patriots in Indianapolis for the third time in four games dating back to the 2006–07 AFC Championship Game.

Instead of dropping the Colts to 8–1 and advancing to 7–2 themselves, the Pats fell to 6–3 while their rivals remained unbeaten.

And the critics took aim at Belichick.

NFL.com columnist Vic Carucci called the choice to pursue first down "one of the all-time goofiest decisions an NFL coach can make." *Sports Illustrated*'s Peter King wrote that the call "smacked of I'm-smarter-than-they-are hubris." Former Patriot Tedy Bruschi sat in the ESPN studio and claimed the call revealed that Belichick lacked confidence in his defense.

The truth of the matter was that Belichick was playing the odds. As football stats analysts across the board pointed out in the days following the game, the Patriots stood a much better chance of converting the fourth down than they did of stopping an offense—*any offense*—from scoring after a punt at that point in the game.

Moreover, as Aaron Schatz, president of Football Outsiders, points out, aggressive play calling on fourth down by and large produces positive results.

"We have what we call our Aggressiveness Index, where we track how often a team goes for it on fourth down," Schatz says. "The three coaches that rank the highest are the three Bills: Parcells, Belichick, and Cowher. What do we know about those guys? Between them, they have six Super Bowl rings as head coach."

"You can argue that going for it *may have* been a mistake," Schatz says. "What you can't argue is that it was definitely a mistake."

> **I**t is ridiculous the way every commentator for the rest of the football season called every stupid decision by any football coach Belichick-like.
>
> —**AARON SCHATZ, FOOTBALL OUTSIDERS**

As it worked out, neither the call nor the result amounted to much. The outcome of the game may have been upsetting, but it became clear very soon afterward that even if the Patriots had won, it wouldn't have made them an elite team. And the Colts, while good enough to squeak by New England, ultimately weren't good enough to win it all either.

The truth about both teams was made clear by the New Orleans Saints, who bulldozed the Pats on *Monday Night Football* in Week 12 and dispatched the Colts on the big stage of Super Bowl XLIV.

Eventually, the fourth-and-two play will be forgotten—by those who agreed with the call and those who decried it—regardless of how momentous it may have seemed at the time. Because the fact is, it wasn't momentous. Not even a little bit.

# Game Details

## New England Patriots 34 • Indianapolis Colts 35

| Patriots | 7 | 17 | 0 | 10 | **34** |
|---|---|---|---|---|---|
| Colts | 7 | 7 | 0 | 21 | **35** |

**Date:** November 15, 2009
**Team Records:** Patriots 6–3; Colts 9–0
**Scoring Plays:**
IND Addai 15-yard pas from Manning (Stover PAT)
NE Maroney 1-yard run (Gostkowski PAT)
NE Gostkowski 31-yard FG
NE Moss 63-yard pass from Brady (Gostkowski PAT)
NE Edelman 9-yard pass from Brady (Gostkowski PAT)
IND Wayne 20yard pass from Manning (Stover PAT)
NE Moss 5-yard pass from Brady (Gostkowski PAT)
IND Garcon 29-yard pass from Manning (Stover PAT)
NE Gostkowski 36-yard FG
IND Addai 4-yard run (Stover PAT)
IND Wayne 1-yard pass from Manning (Stover PAT)

# That Smarts

What was stunning about the Patriots' lone game in the 2009–10 postseason wasn't that the team lost. The days of postseason perfection for the Belichick-Brady–era Pats had been left behind in Denver four years earlier. And it was clear before the playoffs began that New England was too flawed a team to achieve any kind of real success, what with a defense that lacked veteran leadership and an offense that was missing Wes Welker—who tore up his knee in the final game of the regular season—and not getting the best of Randy Moss, who had separated a shoulder in Week 5. It wasn't even that the defeat by the Baltimore Ravens came in Foxborough, where the Pats hadn't lost a postseason game since 1978. The real shocker was that the Patriots were never even in the game. They effectively lost on the first play from scrimmage, when Ravens running back Ray Rice waltzed through a gaping hole in the middle of the Patriots' line and ran untouched 83 yards to put six points on the board. Three plays later, Tom Brady surrendered a fumble on the Patriots' 17-yard line; and when the Ravens converted that turnover to a 14-point lead, the teams might as well have left the field and saved everyone a lot of time, energy, and frustration. Brady threw three picks that day. The Ravens racked up 268 yards of offense, 234 of them on the ground. And Baltimore came out ahead by a score of 33–14.

Ravens running back Ray Rice's 83-yard touchdown on the first play from scrimmage effectively ended the 2009 Patriots' postseason hopes. *Photo courtesy of AP Images.*

# Sources

Associated Press. "Buffalo Victor Against Patriots, Weather." December 21, 1964.

Associated Press. "Patriots Spill Buffalo 14–3." December 5, 1966,

Associated Press. "Patriots Stun Bowl Champion Dolphins." September 16, 1974.

Borges, Ron. "A Get-Rich-Quick Scheme Fails." *The Boston Globe*, January 29, 2006.

Eskenazi, Gerald. "Steelers Lose Gamble, but Win Game Anyway." *The New York Times*, January 4, 1998.

Glennon, Sean. *The Good, the Bad, and the Ugly: Heart-Pounding, Jaw-Dropping, and Gut-Wrenching Moments from New England Patriots History*. Chicago: Triumph Books, 2008.

Glennon, Sean. *This Pats Year: A Trek Through a Season as a Football Fan*. Lanham, MD: Taylor Trade Publishing, 2004.

Hyldburg, Bob. *Total Patriots*. Chicago: Triumph Books, 2009.

Kenyon, Paul. "Patriots Rally to Defeat Chargers in Overtime." *Providence Journal*, October 14, 2001.

Kenyon, Paul. "Trick Play Proves to Be Real Treat for Brady." *Providence Journal*, December 23, 2001.

Miller, Jeffrey J. *Rockin' the Rockpile: The Buffalo Bills of the American Football League*. Toronto, Ontario, Canada: ECW Press, 2007.

Terrell, Roy. "The New Pros Open Up." *Sports Illustrated*, September 12, 1960.

United Press International, "Patriots Raise Division Flag Over Foxboro." December 11, 1978.

Wallace, William N. "Passing of Kemp Gains 286 Yards." *The New York Times*, December 21, 1964.

Wood, Skip. "Loss Hurts Pats' Push for AFC Edge." *USA Today*, December 21, 2004.

Wojciechowski, Gene. "Patriots Pounce on Mistake Prone Jets." *The Los Angeles Times*, December 29, 1985.

Zimmerman, Paul. "A Wild Ride for the Wild Cards." *Sports Illustrated*, January 26, 1986.

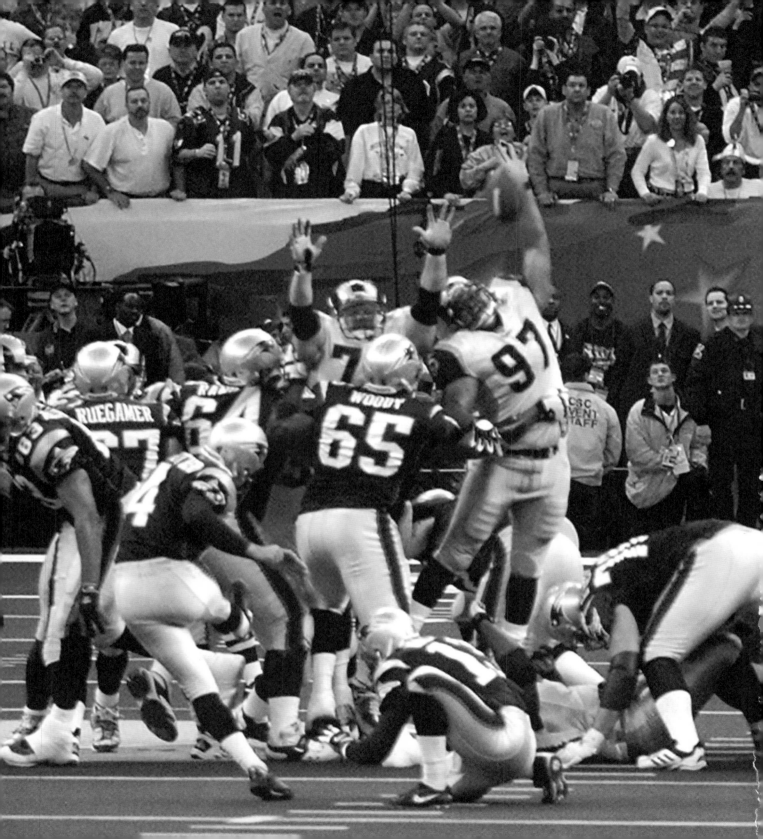